The Creation of the Green Party of the United States

The Creation of the Green Party of the United States

... And Its Neglect of a Strategic Dilemma

by Alan F. Zundel

The Creation of the Green Party of the United States
Copyright © Jan. 2018, Dec. 2020 Alan F. Zundel

Second edition (revised and expanded with new title). Originally published as a
Kindle e-book in 2018, under the title "A History of the Green Party
in the United States, Part 1: Movement or Party? (1983-1994)."

TABLE OF CONTENTS

PREFACE

I do not claim this is a definitive work on the early history of the Green Party in the United States. It is based on extensive research in published and online materials, but I did no interviews and did not delve into any archives. I did have some email correspondence with John Rensenbrink, one of the key participants in this history, to see if he could clear up one puzzling issue. He not only solved it for me but offered to review and comment on all the chapters. I thank him for his input, and hasten to add that he bears no responsibility for my interpretations of events or any mistakes I've made. He did not review the last three chapters, as they were added later at a time when he was hospitalized.

To the best of my knowledge this is currently the most comprehensive early history of the party available, despite what limitations it may have. I hope someday someone will dig deeper and correct or add to the history as I have presented it.

LIST OF ACRONYMS

1984 and before

ISE – Institute for Social Ecology: An organization based on the social ecology philosophy of Murray Bookchin. Many early Greens in the U.S. were affiliated with the ISE.

CoC – Committees of Correspondence: The first national organization of the U.S. Greens, founded in 1984.

IC – Interregional Committee: A decision-making body of delegates from the various regional affiliates of the CoC. Abolished in a 1991 restructuring.

NECoC – North East Committee of Correspondence: An important regional affiliate in the CoC.

1987-1991

SPAKA – Strategy and Policy Approaches in Key Areas: An official document of the national Green organization developed over the years 1987-1990.

LGN – Left Green Network: An independent organization for leftists created in 1987 to advance their views in the CoC.

GCoC – Green Committees of Correspondence: The CoC as renamed in 1989. (Renamed again in 1991 as "the Greens usa.")

GPOC – Green Party Organizing Committee: A organization independent of the GCoC but in a "cooperating" relationship with it for Greens interested in creating state Green parties. GPOC came out of a Working Group on Electoral Action in 1990 and was folded back into the national Green organization in 1991.

CC – Coordinating Committee: An elected body of seven members to conduct business between meetings of the new 1991 Green Council and serve as national spokespersons of the newly renamed Greens usa.

1992 and after

GPN – Green Politics Network: An independent organization for those building state parties. Created by former GPOC members in 1992.

G/GPUSA – The Greens/Green Party USA: New 1992 name of the national Green organization, changed from "the Greens usa."

NIPN – The National Independent Politics Network: An organization that grew out of Ron Daniel's 1992 run for President and engaged in efforts to build an independent political force outside of the two dominant political parties.

ASGP – The Association of State Green Parties: A new national Green Party organization founded just after the Presidential election of 1996.

GPUS – The Green Party of the United States: The ASGP renamed itself the Green Party of the United States in 2001. It is recognized by the Federal Elections Commission as the national committee of the state Green Parties in the U.S.

RCV – Ranked choice voting, also known as instant runoff voting. A voting system that allows voters to rank candidates for an office and helps to lessen the possibility of "spoiler" elections.

CHAPTER ONE

A Personal Overview

The Green Party of the United States was once a promising new political party that rose to national recognition within twelve years of the founding of its parental organization, only to be knocked back and stymied from further progress. Now as then, many American voters are eager for alternatives to the Democrats and the Republicans. I was an active member of the party for two years in California and three years in Oregon, where I became an officer of its Oregon affiliate as well as one of its candidates for statewide public office. My experiences in the party raised the questions which led me to research its early history and resulted in this book. Foremost among those questions was whether the founders had a plan to avoid the political marginalization that alternative parties[1] in the U.S. almost always succumb to. I offer my answer in the concluding chapter. As hinted in the title of this book, it is a negative one, but it demands an explanation. The story of the party's creation provides the grounds for my explanation.

---

[1] The common terms "major" and "minor" parties are value-laden terms that contribute to the institutionalized marginalization of all but two political parties. I prefer to call the so-called major parties "dominant parties" because they use their advantages to maintain a dominant position in the political system. I use the term "alternative parties" for parties other than the two dominant parties.

As my personal political journey illustrates the historical currents that led to the formation of the party, permit me some further autobiography to set the background for its creation and early growth. For it was people very much like me, coming of age in the latter half of the 20th century, who gave the party its character.

I was born in Detroit, Michigan, in the early 1950s, growing up in a working class suburb a few miles outside the city limits. As a boy I was aware that Eisenhower was President, probably from hearing my parents discuss the news over dinner, but politics was not an important topic in our household. That changed when John F. Kennedy ran for President in 1960, my earliest memory of a political campaign. We were Catholics and I'm sure that played a part in my parents' excitement over Kennedy, but it became clear to me that we were also Democrats. This is unsurprising, as both of my parents' families were hard hit by the Great Depression, and they must have remembered Franklin Roosevelt as the benefactor of working people. Somehow I absorbed the belief that government was meant to help people, and that the Democrats were the ones who made sure it did.

Kennedy's successor after his assassination, Lyndon Johnson, was also one of the good guys, not a "nut" (my mother's word) like Barry Goldwater, his Republican rival in the 1964 election. My parents even approved of Johnson signing the civil rights and voting rights laws of the mid-'60s that Martin Luther King, Jr. succeeded in getting on the national agenda. Such policies affirmed their belief in fairness for all people and love-thy-neighbor Christian good will. They were not overt racists like one of my uncles, who had outspoken contempt for "the niggers."

Yet in hindsight there was a subtle racism in my upbringing, one which regarded "colored people" as different and other than us. Racist jokes and mimicry were not unusual, and it was understood that they should live in their own neighborhoods. This outlook boiled over with the racial unrest of the later 1960s. I was staying with my grandmother in Detroit during the summer of 1967 when one of the worst racial uprisings in American history took place just a few miles from us. After that complaints about "those people" ruining the city were unvarnished. I found such statements jarring, puzzling over the incongruity between my Christian upbringing and the hostility and condescension toward black people I heard from the adults around me.

The political world I grew up in shifted after that. During the 1968 Presidential campaign my uncle supported George Wallace, the demagogic champion of racial segregation, with his new American Independent Party breaking from the Democrats. I could also sense my father's movement toward Republican Richard Nixon and his call for law and order, a code phrase for cracking down on restive minorities and protesters. The Democratic coalition of Roosevelt's New Deal was shattering, the old party loyalties dying. (Macomb County, where we lived, was ground zero for the emergence of "Reagan Democrats" among the white working class a decade later, a continuation of this trend.)

As I soon discovered, the political fault line was not only racial, it was generational. Being a teenager in the 1960s meant being exposed to anti-war and anti-Establishment themes via popular music, and by my senior year of high school I had become immersed in the counterculture. I helped publish an underground school newspaper influenced by the student democracy movement and on approaching draft age began paying more attention to political issues. I took part in protests against the Vietnam War and scanned some of the radical pamphlets and newspapers that were handed out, exposing me to a range of leftist political ideas from Marxist sectarianism to the New Left. Near the end of my senior year I also witnessed my school's celebration of the first Earth Day, which kicked off a mass environmental movement modeled on the civil rights and anti-war movements.

By the time I graduated high school, what were eventually to become the Four Pillars of Green Party values were converging in the political views of people like me:

1. Social Justice, with an emphasis on civil rights, human equality and an economy that valued people over profits;

2. Nonviolence, encompassing an anti-war orientation with nonviolent means of political expression;

3. Grassroots Democracy, favoring local organization and people power over top-down authority; and

4. Ecology, from environmental protection to a deeper ecological outlook and rethinking our relationship with the natural world.

In 1972 I cast my first vote for President, favoring Democrat George McGovern, a progressive opponent of the war in Vietnam who was crushed at the ballot box by incumbent Richard Nixon. This defeat was disillusioning for young people, much as Bernie Sanders' loss of the Democratic Presidential nomination was disillusioning to the young people of 2016. Nixon's escalation of the war, contrary to his campaign promises, and the later revelations of his role in obstructing justice in the Watergate investigation, solidified my distrust of the political establishment.

Although I was unaware of it at the time, 1972 was also the year that the Socialist Party of America finally dissolved, splintering into marginalized groups mostly absorbed within the politics of the Democratic Party. The consequence was that heading toward the 1980s there was no established, mass-based, anti-war left wing alternative party in the U.S. for people like me to turn to. The Socialist Party had been crippled by vigorous government repression during World War I and a factional split producing the Communist Party in the 1930s, with yet more serious attrition when the rising wage levels of the 1950s and '60s tamped down economic dissatisfactions. Yet even as the once influential party disappeared, the economic fortunes of working people were undergoing a profound reversal.

I didn't know much about the Socialist Party, but I did know that the economy was changing. I was not especially attentive to politics during the

'70s once the Vietnam War ended. My interests turned toward filmmaking and then to spirituality and intentional communities, and I took up meditation along with the view that true social change depended upon inner change. But being from the Detroit area I couldn't help but know about the problems of the auto industry. Saudi Arabia led an oil embargo that spiked gas prices, and competition from Japanese low-mileage cars caught the complacent American companies off-guard. The economy was going global.

National politicians were in confusion over how to manage the new economy of the 1970s. The old policy tools no longer seemed to be working. Inflation and recession were happening simultaneously and wage levels stopped rising, families staying afloat at first by sending record numbers of women into the work force. In 1976 conservative Southerner Jimmy Carter defeated more liberal contenders in the Democratic primaries by running as a Washington outsider, promising an engineer's practical approach to government and the economy. The New Deal politics of Roosevelt and Johnson was rejected, not only by the Republicans, but now by the Democrats.

When it came time to vote I tried to figure out where I stood, opposed to the Republicans but not thrilled with the Democrats either. I voted for Carter, but for other offices I seriously considered alternative party candidates and may have voted for a few. The Libertarians were attractive for their skepticism toward government, and the Socialist Party USA, a tiny offshoot of the old Socialist Party, for its opposition to big business. But I didn't feel like anyone really spoke to young people and our concerns.

A few years later I was living in the inner city of Detroit, working at a church helping poor residents of the neighborhood, when the economy slumped into yet another recession. The line for food bags at the church tripled and people pleaded for other kinds of help. I organized a meeting in the neighborhood to assess what the greatest needs were and how we could help provide for them. "We need jobs, Alan," was the consensus. How are jobs created? Why do they disappear? What does politics have to do with it? I needed answers to questions that were more complex than I had assumed.

Ronald Reagan won the Presidential election of 1980 in a three-way race against Jimmy Carter and a significant independent bid by John Anderson, the continuation of a movement of voters away from the two dominant parties. The advent of "Reaganomics" served to escalate the national debate about economic policy. I was working on a long-delayed college degree at the University of Detroit, a Jesuit Catholic college, and learning about the social justice themes of the Bible, Catholic social thought, and the Liberation Theology coming out of Latin America. My former belief in social change through inner change was amended: inner change should inspire efforts for social change; they are complementary. While nearing the end of my degree I took several classes in political science. I was searching for an intellectual framework to find my bearings amid this national turn from liberalism to conservatism, and read up on the ideas of non-violent activists like Mohandas Gandhi, Dorothy Day, and Martin Luther King, Jr.

After graduating I was accepted into the graduate program in political science at nearby Wayne State University, where I studied political philosophy, with classes on theories of social justice, the history of Progressivism, and socialist political thought. In the latter class the professor asked what question each of us wanted to answer by taking the class. I said, "Where does the left go from here?" He shook his head. "Lots of people would like to know that."

I don't think either of us knew that during the previous year, 1984, local Green political organizations were beginning to take shape in various parts of the country, inspired by the example of the new European Green Parties. A Green Movement Committee kicked off a meeting to create a national organization, and the committee set as one of its goals that of creating a base of support from "natural allies concerned with ecological politics and social justice, peace and non-violence, local and regional self-management and grassroots democracy." They were describing me, but we hadn't found each other yet.

While working on my master's degree I became particularly interested in "self-managed" economic systems, the very topic mentioned in the Green Movement statement, and wrote my thesis on workplace democracy. At the time there was a lot of union interest in saving the dying industrial cities of the Midwest through workers' buyouts of the factories that were shutting down. Failing to find a career direction after my Master's degree and now with a wife and two young children to support, I accepted a fellowship offer from the University of Michigan to begin work on a doctorate in political science.

I continued to study alternative economic models along with traditional political science topics and got some additional organizing experience in the graduate employees' union. Meanwhile newly minted Green affiliates in various states started winning local offices and running candidates for higher offices in a few places, and I became aware of them as one of the several smaller political parties in our nation. But my political science training also made me aware of how difficult our electoral system made it for alternative parties to get anywhere. I saw the Greens as fated to be marginal political actors.

Then in 1992 Bill Clinton's first Presidential campaign raised the hopes of Democrats, gambling that his promised "third way" would forge a path ahead after twelve years with a Republican in the White House. Between him, incumbent George H.W. Bush and the erratic Ross Perot (another portent of the growing numbers of disaffected voters), Clinton was the easy pick for me. As soon as he was elected, however, he abandoned his campaign promise of policies aiding the middle class in deference to the interests of Wall Street. I had written my doctoral dissertation on the history of U.S. antipoverty policy and was working as a political science professor in Nevada when Clinton signed a conservative welfare reform bill in 1996. That was the last straw. I voted for the Green's first Presidential candidate, Ralph Nader, in that year's Presidential election.

Casting my protest vote felt liberating, but I was not yet ready to leave the Democrats. In 2000 I voted for Al Gore, even though I knew he would continue Clinton's corporate-friendly policies, out of concern that voting for Nader again might allow my state's electoral votes to go to Republican George W. Bush. Yet I knew too much about Presidential elections to buy the simplistic storyline that Nader had cost Gore the election. If anyone was responsible for Gore's loss, Bill Clinton, Al Gore, and the U.S. Supreme Court would be at the top of the list.[2] I chafed at the way the political system inhibited me from voting for my true preference, and sometime during this period I looked into joining the Green Party. Not realizing there were two national organizations I joined one temporarily, but found its newsletter to be too saturated in sectarian socialist rhetoric. Later I discovered it was a small offshoot of a divided Green Party movement.

My dissatisfaction with the Democrats continued to grow. During my time as a professor I was increasingly concerned about the growing economic inequality in the nation, the result of the ongoing economic changes I had been observing since the 1970s. I also saw that neither of the two dominant parties was addressing this issue in any convincing way. My turning point came when I discovered the concept of instant runoff voting while reading a graduate student's master's thesis. Instant runoff voting, now more commonly known as ranked choice voting, is a voting method which if adopted would make alternative parties more viable by reducing the possibility of a "spoiler" election. After the 2000 election a movement to institute instant runoff voting had picked up steam in various parts of the nation, with Green Party members highly involved. When I left academia in 2004 and moved my family to California I did two things: I joined a group working to institute instant runoff voting,[3] and I registered as a Green Party voter.

And that is how my path converged with that of the Green Party. I'm sure many others could share stories that, while differing in details, are similar in that—whether baby boomer, millennial, or in between—you discover

---

[2] For more on the 2000 Presidential election, see the concluding chapter.

[3] Since then a recently developed voting method, STAR Voting, has caught my attention as an improvement over ranked choice voting. See the concluding chapter.

that the political values you hold are the same as those professed by the Green Party. Once you become aware of this, you either slowly or more rapidly realize: this party gives voice to my political views, under a government that tries to suppress that voice and limit my voting choices.

Here is the story of the founders' struggle to free our voice and expand our democratic choices.

Alan F. Zundel

CHAPTER TWO

The German Spark

Jay Walljasper was depressed and discouraged. He worked at the newspaper *In These Times*, a democratic socialist bi-weekly based in Chicago, and by 1983 the Reagan Revolution had taken hold of the country. Neoconservatives were in charge of the administration and Republicans controlled the U.S. Senate. Liberals couldn't muster up much of an alternative vision, other than "reopening a few steel mills, bolstering the membership of a few unions, and increasing monthly payments to welfare mothers." Reporting the news had become "a bleak task."

Then something unexpected came across his desk. European correspondent Diana Johnstone reported on a new left wing political party in West Germany, one whose electoral prospects looked surprisingly good for the upcoming elections. The platform of *Die Grünen* (the Green Party) was based on the values of nonviolence, grassroots democracy, ecology, and feminism, and their policy proposals were daring: nuclear disarmament, organic farming, dismantling nuclear power plants, and the redistribution of wealth. But unlike the traditional socialist or liberal programs, they wanted to return political and economic power to local communities. To Walljasper it sounded too good to be true.

It wasn't. A few weeks later the Greens won twenty-seven seats in West

Germany's national parliament, garnering 5.6% of the vote and becoming the first new party to enter the legislature since 1953. This was a proverbial shot heard 'round the world, inspiring Green Parties to emerge in nations all over the globe.

Walljasper wasn't the only American latching on to news of the German Greens. German scholar Herbert Kitschelt recounts that when he began lecturing on West German parties in the United States in the early '80s, his academic hosts and graduate students in political science "favored no theme as much as the rise and future of the German Greens." And this was before they had won any seats in the national parliament. Editors of the *New York Times* found dispatches on the German Greens of sufficient interest to readers to publish forty-seven articles prior to the 1983 election. With the electoral success of '83, media attention really exploded.

The hook for many people was that the party was aligned with the values of the new social movements, such the student democracy and anti-war movements of the 1960s and the environmental and feminist movements of the 1970s. A whole generation had been shaped by these movements, both in Europe and the United States. They were tired of the old politics of the traditional parties and hungering for something new, something that both matched their values and had a realistic chance at cracking entrenched political systems. The German Greens showed that this was no dream, it was actually possible.

The German party was neither the first nor the only Green Party popping up at the time. The pattern is very similar across many Western nations. Environmental groups formed in the late 1960s and early '70s, with governments at first being somewhat responsive to their concerns. Then with the economic difficulties of the 1970s politicians set environmental issues to the side. In response the groups turned to protest tactics and an adversarial position toward their governments, followed by the forming of coalitions to run candidates of their own for offices. Soon they built alliances with other "outsider" groups to form political parties, focusing first on local and regional elections. Finally the parties adopted the Green label, which was becoming recognizable across Europe and beyond.

Because this process developed in different stages in different countries, it is hard to say where the first Green Party was established. For example, the Values Party of New Zealand was founded in 1972 and is sometimes claimed as the first national party based on environmental issues, yet it only adopted the Green Party name after reorganization in 1990. In a similar example the PEOPLE Party was formed in England in 1972, changing its name to the Ecology Party in 1975 and the Green Party in 1985. By the early 1980s environmentally-oriented parties had developed throughout most of the Western democracies, including Australia, Sweden, Ireland, Portugal, the Netherlands, Switzerland, France, and Canada. Now they are found around the world under the Green Party banner, including North and South America, Eastern Europe, Africa, Asia, and the Middle East.

Belgium was actually the first Green Party to win seats in their national parliament. It had two Green parties, each for a different language group, which worked jointly and in 1981 won four seats with 4.8% of the vote. They arrived at the opening session of parliament riding bicycles as a symbolic gesture against modern society's reliance on fossil fuels. When the West Germans won their seats in 1983, they mirrored the Belgians by carrying into their opening session a dead tree withered by acid rain. The Finland Greens also won a couple seats in their 1983 national elections. The following year Luxemburg won two seats in theirs and both the Belgian and West German Greens elected representatives to the European Parliament.

So why was it the German Greens' 1983 election which gained so much attention? Most likely because Germany is such a prominent nation and the number of candidates they elected to their parliament was relatively large. The evolution of the German Greens followed the usual pattern. The genesis of the party can be found in the late '60s protest movements seeking more citizens' input into the decisions of government. In the mid-'70s scattered environmental groups consolidated against the slow pace of reform and the continued threats to the environment, especially nuclear power plants. By 1977 they were networking with peace, women's, socialist and other groups to support candidates in elections, at first local and then regional. *Die Grünen* was founded in January 1980 in anticipation of federal elections that fall. They won 1.5% of the vote in that election, which was significant because any party winning more than a half-percent received a per vote reimbursement for campaign expenses. These funds helped them continue to build toward their eventual electoral achievement of March '83.

Could the United States follow the same path as these European nations?

Charlene Spretnak of California was on a lecture tour in West Germany the previous year when she became interested in the Greens. Spretnak was typical of the baby boomers delving into the "new" spiritual movements of the time. Born in Pittsburg in 1946, she grew up in a Catholic family in Ohio but lost her faith while attending a Jesuit university. She drifted in and out of graduate school and eventually made a pilgrimage to India, where she took up Buddhist Vipassana meditation. Afterward she settled in California to finish her degree and research women's spirituality, in which the sacredness of nature plays an essential role. She had published two books by 1982, *Lost Goddesses of Early Greece* (1978) and *The Politics of Women's Spirituality* (1981). Spretnak was intrigued not only by the Greens' affinity with the values and issues of the new political movements, but by the occasional mention in their writings of the "spiritual impoverishment" of modern society.

Her friend Fritjof Capra, author of *The Tao of Physics* (1975), also did a lecture tour in West Germany that year and shared Spretnak's interest. Back in the U.S. they followed media coverage of the Greens over the course of the year, which eventually inspired Spretnak to set aside her other projects and ask Capra to write a book proposal with her. They interviewed and researched the Greens while in West Germany for new lecture tours;

Spretnak's tour was in June 1983, a few months after the historic election. On returning home they presented their research in various forums as they worked on their book, constantly encountering people eager to see an American Green Party. These hopes were further stirred up by a fall 1983 U.S. lecture tour by leaders from the German Greens.

In April 1984 Spretnak and Capra published their book, *Green Politics*, which not only discussed Green political thinking but outlined ideas for an American organization for Green politics. The book galvanized readers across the United States, with letters and phone calls pouring in from people all over the nation expecting them to make this happen. Capra declined a leadership role, but Spretnak reluctantly ventured into the forefront of the rapidly developing movement to create a Green political organization in the United States.

Across the country in Augusta, Maine, activists from the environmental, peace, and alternative economics movements were doing just that, having already held an organizing meeting for a state Green Party—the first Green political organization in the United States. One of the two conveners was John Rensenbrink, a scholar like Spretnak but more political activist than spiritual seeker.

Rensenbrink was of the pre-baby boomer generation, having been born in 1928 and raised in Pease, Minnesota. His ailing father kept him from high school to assist with the family dairy farm, but his mother helped him enroll in a correspondence course without his father's knowledge. When his father died of cancer Rensenbrink and his brother, both in their teens, were left to run the farm. His interest in politics was stoked when the *Minneapolis Star Journal* published his letter of youthful praise for the progressive Republican Harold Stassen, the governor of Minnesota, who later ran for President three times. Further letters to the editor were also published and the historical novel *Raintree County* became an additional source of patriotic inspiration to him. Rensenbrink was barely accepted on probation into Calvin College in

Grand Rapids, Michigan, which was unimpressed with his correspondence diploma, but he became a star student as well as editor of the weekly school paper. He went on to earn graduate degrees in political science from the University of Michigan and the University of Chicago and taught at various colleges, finally settling with his wife Carla Washburn in mid-coastal Maine to teach at Bowdoin College. In the mid-to-late '60s he founded a regional anti-poverty program in Maine, was a leader in protests against the Vietnam War, and helped organize and chaired a group to reform the Maine Democratic Party. In the 1970s he twice ran for the Democratic nomination to the state senate, losing both times, and later helped lead the campaign to shut down the Maine Yankee nuclear power plant.

Rensenbrink heard about the election of the German Greens while on a five month research trip to Poland in 1983 to study the Solidarity movement. On his way home that summer he stopped to learn more from some German friends who had joined the party. When Rensenbrink got back to the U.S. a fellow anti-nuclear activist, Alan Philbrook, called to say he'd been to the first meeting of Greens in Canada and on returning had registered a Green Party of Maine. The two friends called a meeting of activists for January 14th, 1984 and, despite a recent major snowstorm, seventeen people showed up to found the Maine Green Party/Movement. The group met again in February to start the process of writing procedures and a policy platform, with a dual focus on Green values and building an independent party. Rensenbrink later said of his motivations:

> The environment was virtually without a voice in politics. Social justice was lagging terribly. Democracy and equality seemed to be losing out. War was becoming the chief preoccupation of the 'military Congressional industrial complex,' and top politicians of both parties followed suit. The country needed a political jolt, a shot in the arm. In American history that has usually been provided by a new party.

A few months later, in May of 1984—a month after Spretnak and Capra's book appeared—the first North American Bio-Regional Congress was held in the Ozark foothills in Missouri, sponsored by a network of individuals and groups devoted to ecology, bio-regionalism, organic farming, holistic health, political ecology, and related subjects. David Haenke, an organizer of the conference, had invited Spretnak to speak at the Congress. In her talk she managed to overcome suspicion toward Green politics as a potential competitor to the bio-regionalist movement, inspiring some of the attendees to form a Green Movement Committee. The committee approved a statement on the development of a U.S. Green political organization, saying in part:

> As individual bio-regionalists, we recognize the need for bio-regional principles and practices to be secured and protected, co-operatively and in a decentralized manner, through a Green political organization. Such an organization should focus on open, democratic planning and political action supportive of local and regional autonomy and interdependence as reflected in the bio-regional model.
>
> To be effective, a Green political organization must originate from a broad base of support, from natural allies concerned with ecological politics and social justice, peace and non-violence, local and regional self-management and grassroots democracy. If the emerging Green political organization does indeed reflect these basic bio-regional concerns, we urge support from bio-regional groups and individuals from around the continent.

The statement was well received at the Congress, and later that summer Spretnak, Haenke, democratic socialist author Harry Boyte, Gloria Goldberg of the Institute for Social Ecology (ISE) in Vermont, and Earth Bank co-founder Catherine Burton in Seattle, each of them from a different region of the country, established an organizing committee. They subsequently invited 200 social change groups to send representatives knowledgeable in one or more of twenty-seven issue areas to a meeting in St. Paul, Minnesota later that year. Most of the groups did not reply, but a few dozen did send someone, while Burton managed to raise $10,000 to help some attendees with airfare to the event. Sixty-two people arrived the weekend of August 10th-12th to establish the first national Green organization in the United States.

But not a political party. There was a long, hard road ahead of them before they got to that point.

CHAPTER THREE

The First Founding

In one of history's ironies, the last national convention of the soon-to-be-defunct Citizens Party was held elsewhere in St. Paul that same August 1984 weekend. The delegates at the Citizens Party convention adopted a platform modelled on that of the British Ecology Party, which changed its name to the Green Party the following year. The delegates also nominated Sonja Johnson for U.S. President. When Johnson ended up throwing her support to Democrat Walter Mondale, the irrelevance of the party was unmistakable. The Citizens Party was one of a series of attempts to create a new party independent of the Democrats and Republicans during the 1960s and '70s. These included the Freedom Now Party, the Mississippi Freedom Democratic Party, La Raza Unida and the People's Party. All failed either to tie disparate social movements together or to have an impact on national politics, soon reverting back to direct action activity or attempts to influence the Democrats. The American two-party system propped up by our election laws has long been a difficult nut to crack. Without a system of proportional representation like many European nations have, new parties find it next to impossible to win the legislative seats needed to build credibility and escape marginalization.

Not that creating a new party was a shared purpose of the other gathering in St. Paul. A significant number of those who descended upon "the leafy campus of Macalester College" for the Green politics meeting had no interest in creating a political party. The aims and views of the attendees varied considerably. As one commentator put it, they drew from across a political spectrum from "anarchists to electoralists," the former out to dismantle government power while the latter wanted to take a seat in it. There were activists from the peace, environmental, women's, and civil rights movements; anarchists, socialists and deep ecologists; farmers, teachers, and church and community leaders. "Bioregionalists sat down with capitalists, libertarians with world order advocates," observed Mark Satin, a participant/journalist for his newsletter *New Options*.

Against this narrative of diversity, attendee Howie Hawkins[4] later described the assembly as "more New Age than New Left" and "virtually all upper middle-class and white," noting that writers and academics outnumbered grassroots activists. He also alleged that the Maine Green Party/Movement had not been invited specifically because they had intended to form a political party. Another writer also affirms this, laying the responsibility for the non-invitation on bio-regionalists from Maine. Later events made it clear not only that bio-regionalists like Haenke were opposed to creating a political party, but Harry Boyte and social ecologists like Gloria Goldberg were also opposed. Eleven members from the organization she was affiliated with, the ISE, showed up despite the two-person-per-organization limit in the invitation, and they were uniformly against creating a national party. Spretnak later wrote of them accusingly, "a small anti-party group crashed the founding conference and blocked all efforts to form a national Green Party." This was a harbinger of what was to become a major rift in the new organization.

Whatever the differences or similarities of the participants, they did manage to accomplish three things. One, they set up a structure for fostering

---

[4] Yes, this is the same Howie Hawkins who was the Green Party's Presidential candidate in 2020. He will play a leading role in our story.

and connecting local Green groups. Two, they chose a name. And three, they developed a set of guiding principles.

Much discussion was taken up with what exactly they were there to create. Catherine Burton argued for a computer network, "a network and not an organization," to spread individual ecological consciousness by direct democratic communications. As personal computers were at that time the province of a sub-culture, this idea did not go far. Spretnak, Haenke, Boyte and Satin backed the idea of a traditional staff-based organization with dues-paying members and experts on relevant topics educating the public via newsletters and other media. Opponents complained that such a centralized organization would become unaccountable to the base. Dan Chodorkoff, director of the ISE, instead proposed a confederation of grassroots local groups which would send representatives to a temporary body until local organizing had taken root and a broader group of participants could have input on the structure.

In the end the latter position won out, although the advocates of the more centralized structure repeatedly revived the debate over the course of the meeting. The interim body of representatives from local groups was titled the Interregional Committee (IC), with a planned central Clearing House intended to facilitate fund raising, communications and the dissemination of literature. The IC was to meet three times a year to oversee the Clearing House and assist with educational events for local and regional development. Representation would be by one male and one female selected by each of the regional organizations around the country, starting with seven or eight "more or less bio-regionally defined" areas. In keeping with the democratic spirit of recent decades with their collectives, communes and cooperatives, decisions of the IC were to be made by a consensus-seeking process.

Dissension over political ideology broke to the surface while discussing a location for the Clearing House. Spretnak suggested the Northeast, as there was something of an organizational base there in the ISE. Mark Satin, having had unpleasant encounters with members of the ISE in the past, refused to agree to this until the Northeast Caucus made its political views explicit, declaring that "the Green movement should not be associated with the Institute for Social Ecology and Murray Bookchin." Bookchin, born in New York City in 1921, was a longtime socialist activist and the influential author of several books developing his theory of social ecology, which combined ecological concepts with an anarchist[5] socialist political vision. Chodorkoff, who had founded the ISE with Bookchin, accused Satin of sowing divisiveness by red-baiting socialists. Harry Boyte intervened with an offer to host the Clearing House in St. Paul, and both sides agreed to this compromise.

Choosing a name also proved contentious. Surprisingly, given the origins of the meeting, some people objected to the use of the word "Green" in the name of the national organization. The argument was that for minority communities it signaled middle-class concern over the environment to the neglect of social issues. (Civil rights activist Jesse Jackson was initiating his Rainbow Coalition at the time, thus precipitating comparison with its more encompassing symbol.) Instead, on the suggestion of Boyte, they named their network the "Committees of Correspondence" (CoC) in homage to the name taken by the colonists who fomented the American Revolution. As someone pointed out much later, the name was even less apt for attracting the descendants of enslaved Africans or indigenous Americans. But the idea was that the American revolutionaries had also sought to base themselves on strong local units rather than centralized control. Apparently no one stopped to reflect that after the war some of the revolutionaries regretted the lack of a strong central government and wrote the American Constitution to rectify this. And that years later a bloody Civil War broke out to determine whether states or the central government were to have the last

---

[5] Anarchism, for those who are not versed in the political tradition, is not aimed at sowing chaos and destruction. It holds that state structures relying on coercion have always been instruments of class oppression, and that an inherent human capacity for voluntary cooperation and social organization is suppressed by and underdeveloped due to these structures. Some anarchists have argued that attacking the symbols and agents of the state are a means to draw out its repressive nature and rouse the populace to oppose it. It is this wing of the tradition that gave anarchism its reputation for property destruction and violence.

word in disputes between them. The chosen name definitely reflected some of the meeting's unresolved tensions, whether consciously or not.

Given these tensions you would think the creation of a set of principles would have been a sticking point, but according to Satin's account it was not. Fifty participants were sprawled across a lounge floor for a Saturday evening plenary workshop led by activist Jeff Land. The conference had been intense and exhausting to that point, but there was shared anticipation that something important could come out of this workshop. The aim was to create a statement that would define the group and "put us on the political map." Satin brought up the "Values and Ethics" chapter of his 1974 book, *New Age Politics*. Someone else suggested the Black Panthers' Ten Point Plan of the '60s as a guidepost. Others spoke of the Four Pillars of the German Greens, and someone even brought up an old Populist document. People discussed the values they'd like to see represented while a person wrote the suggestions on a flipchart. According to Satin a "collective brain" seemed to take hold as the meeting continued. By the time twenty suggestions had been recorded, Satin recommended whittling them down to ten, soon dubbed the "Ten Key Values." At some point Jeff Land tired and Satin took over as facilitator until the group finally adjourned.

A less mythic account of how the Ten Key Values were composed was given by Howie Hawkins. He claimed that Satin and Spretnak were the principal authors and circulated drafts throughout the weekend. In building upon the Four Pillars of the German Greens, "ecology" was altered to "ecological wisdom" as a reflection of the "spiritual and mystical bent" that they and other participants shared. "Personal" was adjoined to "social responsibility" to emphasize the importance of "personal transformation," indicating the individual as a locus of change rather than a purely social locus such as class. The additions of "postpatriarchal values" and "respect for diversity" were nods to feminism and racial equality. Greta Gaard later expanded on Hawkins' analysis, arguing that both "postpatriarchal values" and "community-based economics" exhibited aversion to socialist frames of thinking about feminism and economics.

Regardless of the specifics of the process, any cooperative spirit unraveled again after the values workshop ended. To continue the process Satin had invited anyone who wanted to talk about next steps to visit him at a dimly lit table behind the lounge. First up was Charlene Spretnak. Despite their mutual interest in spiritually-grounded politics, relations between the two were testy. Satin had written a "constructively critical" review of *Green Politics* earlier that year and Spretnak had responded with an angry letter and follow-up card. Satin had also made a complaining phone call to Spretnak when he felt that Gloria Goldberg was deliberately keeping him off the invitation list for the meeting. Spretnak marched up to the table with a stern warning to Satin not to "[fuck] things up." Next were the ISE devotees of Murray Bookchin's social ecology. As mentioned earlier, Satin had wrestled with them before and "was sick of it" so presumably this did not go well either. Various other representatives of different wings of the assembly showed up after that, but Satin does not report on whether any of these conversations were more collegial. He just wrote that he was "as prickly as anyone else at the founding meeting."

Satin was to continue on as a participant and reporter of the early Green movement for several years. Born in 1946, he quit college to work with the Student Nonviolent Coordinating Committee in Mississippi. In 1966, while back in college in New York, he became president of a local chapter of the Students for a Democratic Society. Shortly after this he fled to Canada to evade the draft, where he founded a program to aid other Vietnam War resisters and wrote the widely distributed *Manual for Draft-Age Immigrants to Canada* (1968). After the war he delved into the consciousness movement and published *New Age Politics* (1976), identifying a new "third force" in American politics oriented toward simpler lifestyles, decentralism and a sense of global responsibility. He co-founded the New World Alliance to work toward realizing these ideals, but when the organization foundered he took to publishing the *New Options* newsletter as a way to promote social change. Later he was to write of the bickering in these political movements:

> Looking back now after nearly three decades, I feel more empathy for our misbehavior—others' and mine—than I used to. The Cold War was in full bloom; fear and a sense of urgency were our daily bread. Despite our sincere spiritual practices or enjoyable socio-political roles (or both), most of us were working ourselves to exhaustion for social change, most of us still felt rotten for not having stopped the Vietnam War *before over one million people had been slaughtered*, and most of us felt distinctly underappreciated by the society at large. Sometimes even our families looked away. And it wasn't just the Greens. I had experienced thin-skinnedness, barely-disguised competitiveness, and related frailties before—in the ecologically and spiritually minded New World Alliance. Others had experienced similar phenomena in other post-Vietnam groups struggling to be heard.
>
> What's surprising, then—even somewhat miraculous—is not that the Ten Key Values statement failed to take the political arena by storm, but that it got written and distributed at all. Despite our manifold personal and political conflicts, there was enough strength in our souls—fire in our bellies—and love in our hearts—that we were able to create a process that brought the statement into being.

At an open session on the morning of the last day of the St. Paul conference, the group assigned Spretnak and Satin to write a draft of the Ten Key Values with brief descriptions of each. These were to be based on the flip-chart pages and associated conversations along with feedback from the meeting participants over the coming weeks. Spretnak suggested adding Eleanor LeCain to the drafters but Satin objected, having soured on committee work from past political experiences. The group supported Satin but permitted them each to accept help from anyone who was at the founding meeting. Some of the socialist participants had reservations about Satin and the failure to include a more explicitly anti-capitalist position in the Values, but calculated that this would be a working paper subject to further revision.

Those assembled adjourned and everyone went back to their home locales to organize committees to correspond in the new CoC. Spretnak and Satin returned to their respective homes to confront a collection of sometimes contradictory principles which were to be crafted into a compelling statement. They spent countless hours on the phone, she in Berkeley, California, and he in Washington, D.C., trying to give shape and coherence to the statement, with Spretnak covering the long-distance phone bills. More suggestions and policy ideas kept flowing in from colleagues. Spretnak conferred with LeCain in Berkeley while Satin got assistance from Gerald Goldfarb and Robert Theobald. Satin was particularly concerned with avoiding prescriptions and instead inspiring creative thinking with the values statement. A key decision was to look behind the positions being taken to the questions that gave rise to them, and so to frame the values as open-ended questions. The result was the Ten Key Values statement still used by the Green Party of the U.S., although revised somewhat over the years. Their draft was delivered to the IC, which disseminated it throughout the CoC for discussion by the membership. After minor edits the IC approved and released it late in the year. That foundational version reads as follows:

Introduction

This list of values and questions for discussion was composed by a diverse group of people who are working to build a new politics, which has kinship with Green movements around the world. We feel the issues we have raised below are not being addressed adequately by the political left or right. We invite you to join with us in refining our values, sharpening our questions – and translating our perspective into practical and effective political actions.

Ecological Wisdom

How can we operate human societies with the understanding that we are PART of nature, not on top of it? How can we live within the ecological and resource limits of the planet, applying our technological knowledge to the challenge of an energy-efficient economy? How can we build a better relationship between cities and countryside? How can we guarantee the rights of non-human species? How can we promote sustainable agriculture and respect for self-regulating natural systems? How can we further biocentric wisdom in all spheres of life?

Grassroots Democracy

How can we develop systems that allow and encourage us to control the decisions that affect our lives? How can we ensure that representatives will be fully accountable to the people who elected them? How can we develop planning mechanisms that would allow citizens to develop and implement their own preferences for policies and spending priorities? How can we encourage and assist the "mediating institutions" – family, neighborhood organization, church group, voluntary association, ethnic club – to recover some of the functions now performed by government? How can we relearn the best insights from American traditions of civic vitality, voluntary action and community responsibility?

Personal and Social Responsibility

How can we respond to human suffering in ways that promote dignity? How can we encourage people to commit themselves to lifestyles that promote their own health? How can we have a community-controlled education system that effectively teaches our children academic skills, ecological wisdom, social responsibility and personal growth? How can we resolve personal and intergroup conflicts without just turning them over to lawyers and judges? How can we take responsibility for reducing the crime rate in our neighborhoods? How can we encourage such values as simplicity and moderation?

Nonviolence

How can we, as a society, develop effective alternatives to our current patterns of violence at all levels, from the family and the street to nations and the world? How can we eliminate nuclear weapons from the face of the Earth without being naive about the intentions of other governments? How can we most constructively use nonviolent methods to oppose practices and policies with which we disagree, and in the process reduce the atmosphere of polarization and selfishness that is itself a source of violence?

Decentralization

How can we restore power and responsibility to individuals, institutions, communities and regions? How can we encourage the flourishing of regionally-based cultures, as distinct from a dominant monoculture? How can we locate the power of our political, economic and social institutions closer to home in ways that are efficient and practical? How can we reconcile the need for community and regional self-determination with the need for appropriate centralized regulation in certain matters?

Community-Based Economics

How can we redesign our work structures to encourage employee ownership and workplace democracy? How can we develop new economic activities and institutions that will allow us to use our new technologies in ways that are humane, freeing, ecological, and responsive to communities? How can we establish some form of basic economic security, open to all? How can we move beyond the narrow "job ethic" to new definitions of work, jobs and income that reflect the changing economy? How can we change our income distribution pattern to reflect the wealth created by those outside the formal, monetary economy – those who take responsibility for parenting, housekeeping, home gardening, doing community volunteer work, etc.? How can we restrict the size and concentrated power of corporations without discouraging superior efficiency or technological innovation?

Postpatriarchal Values

How can we replace the cultural ethos of dominance and control with more cooperative ways of interacting? How can we encourage people to care about persons outside their own group? How can we promote the building of respectful, positive and responsive relationships across the lines of gender and other divisions? How can we encourage a rich, diverse political culture that respects feelings as well as rationalist approaches? How can we proceed with as much respect for the means as the end, the process as well as the product? How can we learn to respect the contemplative, inner part of life as much as the outer activities?

Respect for Diversity

How can we honor cultural, ethnic, racial, sexual, religious and spiritual diversity within the context of individual responsibility toward all beings? While honoring diversity, how can we reclaim our country's finest shared ideals – the dignity of the individual, democratic participation, and liberty and justice for all?

Global Responsibility

How can we be of genuine assistance to the grassroots groups in the Third World – and what can WE learn from such groups? How can we help other countries make a transition to self-sufficiency in food and other basic necessities? How can we cut our defense budget while maintaining an adequate defense? How can we promote these ten Green values in reshaping our global order? How can we reshape the global order without creating just another enormous nation-state?

Future Focus

How can we induce people and institutions to think in terms of the long-range future, and not just in terms of their short-range selfish interest? How can we encourage people to develop their own visions of the future and move more effectively toward them? How can we judge whether new technologies are socially useful – and use those judgments to shape our society? How can we induce our government and other institutions to practice fiscal responsibility? How can we make the quality of life, rather than open-ended economic growth, the focus of future thinking?

※ ※ ※

The Ten Key Values statement proved to be an invaluable resource for recruitment of members and generating discussion in the local groups as they began organizing. Overall, despite many hands pulling in different directions, the wagon train seemed to be rolling forward. Where exactly it was headed, though, was to remain a controversial question.

CHAPTER FOUR

Fledgling Fights

Rensenbrink's group in Maine knew nothing about the St. Paul assembly, as either the organizers were not aware of or—more likely—had deliberately excluded them. The Maine group had been holding monthly meetings and attracting new members from across the state since their start in January, with co-founder Alan Philbrook "champing at the bit" to get Green parties going in other states. In September they learned of a gathering for people interested in Green politics to be held two days later in Concord, New Hampshire, so "we gathered ourselves together, got in our cars and roared to the meeting. We hadn't been invited. We went anyway." Arriving just after the meeting began, they startled the others by their sudden appearance. It was their turn to be surprised when they heard the news about the formation of the new national Green organization just the previous month. Although "nettled" a bit over not having been invited to the founding assembly—"quite disappointed in fact"—they soon joined via the regional affiliate.

They may not have been the only ones feeling disappointed with the new organization. Even as fresh recruits like the Maine group entered the CoC, others were exiting. Most of those present at the St. Paul meeting never participated in the organization again. Some may have gone over to other groups, such as the North American Green Network, a computer network connecting the like-minded in North America and Europe much as been proposed and rejected in St. Paul. Others may have sniffed out the underlying tensions at the founding meeting and decided to avoid the storm clouds on the horizon. If so, they had good noses: it started pouring right away. Within a few years only about a half dozen of the original group were still active in it.

The first raindrops fell on the Clearing House. Harry Boyte, the compromise candidate to run it, send a letter to his political associates inviting them to join the CoC but warning them of a faction of "anarchist ultra-democrats" within it. (That would be Bookchin and the social ecologists of the ISE.) It was also later discovered that Boyte had rebuffed friendly inquiries from the Citizens Party, Socialist Party USA, and Labor-Farm Party. And at a public meeting in their state, members of the aspiring Maine party heard Boyte emphasize that the CoC was aimed at working within the Democratic Party, not creating an independent one.

The Maine group had been established as a "Party/Movement," a word straining with ambiguity. According to Rensenbrink, immediately after its founding the group had gotten tied up in an argument between "party-types and movement-types." The former were eager to engage in electoral activity as an independent party, but the latter feared this would deflect energy from movement building and get them compromised by the system they wanted to transform. Boyte's pronouncement could only have exacerbated the already touchy situation. The party versus movement conflict was to persist on and off for a stress-filled two years in Maine and cropped up in other regions as well, ultimately to reappear on the national level. According to Greg Gerritt, the Maine group was also riven by a dispute between vegetarians and biodynamic farmers, which blew up the group within a year and a half. The meeting following the blowup had only three participants: Rensenbrink, Gerritt, and Matt Tilley.

When Boyte's activities as the Clearing House coordinator came to light, those he had criticized as a disruptive faction called him to account for it and he soon resigned. Now the IC resumed the fight over how much activity was to be allowed from the national center. Some of the representatives, mostly based in the Northeast, wanted the Clearing House to be just a mail drop and information center without any outreach function to other organizations. Others in the IC complained that this approach hindered the kind of support the Clearing House could offer to new groups or potential groups in various regions.

Behind this seeming administrative debate were differences in political philosophy that the Ten Key Values had papered over. Those who wanted to constrain the Clearing House were against centralized power on principle. Their view was that a more ecologically-based society could only be built on direct action and local electoral tactics, because centralized state and economic power was the main obstacle to political and economic democracy. This was essentially the anarchist socialism of Bookchin and the ISE. Those who wanted a more active role for the Clearing House in coordinating the work of local and regional groups saw electoral activity at all levels, local, state and eventually national, as a path to achieving fundamental change in public policy. In their eyes radical political action was that which is transformative of 'politics as usual,' to be 'neither left nor right but in front,' as the German Greens had put it.

There were also other divisions within the CoC. Those supporting electoral work were divided over whether to create an independent party or focus on reforming the Democratic Party. The bio-regionalists objected to a creating a party because it would entail organizing on the basis of political districts rather than on that of ecological bio-regions. The bio-regionalists also fought with socialists, especially in New York City, over unlikely proposals such as population dispersion for the sake of protecting the ecosystem. All of these cross-cutting political currents sucked the IC into a frustrating whirlpool of protracted debate whenever any decisions needed to be made.

Outside of a few areas such as the Northeast and California, the planned nurturing of local and regional groups was stalled by the struggles in the IC during the year following the founding meeting. Even so, there were encouraging signs of life beginning to sprout.

Early on New England city and regional groups had established the New England Committees of Correspondence (NECoC) and began holding regional assemblies throughout the year. Initially they solicited working papers to stimulate discussions, but by their fourth regional assembly they agreed to move from discussion to action and established three working groups: Renewable Energy/Public Power, Statement of Principles, and one to compile a Green organizing packet.

Some attendees at the January 1985 NECoC assembly in Amherst, Massachusetts decided to form a New Haven Green Party. They adopted a relatively early focus on electoral action and laid plans to run candidates for several offices, including Mayor and Alder seats, in the November election. Their platform included greater democracy (citizen referenda and city budget transparency), environmental issues (nonnuclear power and energy conservation), social justice (tax reform), peace (support for the Nuclear Freeze Campaign and No First Strikes Pledge), and human rights (equal services in all neighborhoods and barring city business with companies that discriminate).

Greens began meeting in the San Francisco Bay area in late '84, and by May of the following year affiliate groups were operating in San Francisco and the East Bay. Charlene Spretnak, her husband Danny Moses, and Jonathan Porritt, a representative of the British Green Party, gave presentations at the founding of the East Bay Green Alliance in Berkeley. In Southern California a group was being organized in Los Angeles around the same time and, as in New Haven, began planning to run candidates for city and county offices in the fall.

A contemporary observer in the spring of 1985 found active groups in over twenty cities. For example, in Vermont several hundred people worked on a common-ground statement to bring different organizations into a coalition under the Green umbrella. Similarly in New York about 1,000 people met over a nine month period to fashion a statement of principles for a coalition to carry out Green projects aimed at making a difference in people's everyday lives. There had been about twenty-five local groups across the country in 1984, a number which doubled during the following year.

In August of 1985, one year after the founding, the national IC met in Boston while the NECoC was also meeting there. The vitality of the New England locals impressed the IC delegates and spurred them to renew efforts to build at the grassroots in their own areas and elsewhere. Activity started to pick up and continued into the following year, during which the number of locals grew from fifty to about eighty. The Greens began to have a noticeable impact.

The New Haven candidates won 10% of the citywide vote and nearly a quarter of the votes where they ran for Alder seats. In five races they came in second, ahead of the Republicans in four and tying them in the fifth. Both the New Haven Greens and the Keene Greens of New Hampshire stopped plans for waste incineration plants. The Boston Greens worked with other groups to devote 200 acres on the grounds of a former mental health hospital to organic farming, an organic food market, and gardening cooperatives. The Maine Greens defeated a ten to one funding disadvantage to beat the opposition and pass a November 1985 referendum requiring plans for nuclear waste disposal to pass a statewide vote. And in December the Northern Vermont Greens successfully opposed a bond issue for a waterfront development backed by independent socialist mayor (and future Presidential candidate) Bernie Sanders, even though the Greens were outspent by twenty-eight to one. They argued Sanders was too focused on jobs and tax revenues at the cost of gentrification and loss of public lands that could be used for a state park.

When the IC met that December in Kansas City, they ratified the growing sentiment that the IC and the Clearing House should actively support local and regional groups with a variety of services. Dee Berry stepped in and volunteered to host the Clearing House in Kansas City. Berry was a feminist critic of binary "either/or" thinking as a foundation of patriarchy, with its superior/inferior, win/lose kind of dichotomies. Instead she promoted a "both/and" outlook to honor diverse views while searching for common ground, a perspective which heartened those who felt caught in the middle of the various internal conflicts. The IC moved the Clearing House to Kansas, where it thrived under Berry's leadership and with the support of Ben Kjelshus. The monthly *IC Bulletin* and quarterly *Green Letter* newsletter, published by the Clearing House and mailed to dues-paying locals, became key sources for news articles publicizing CoC projects around the country.

And news there certainly was: in the spring of '86 the U.S. Greens had their first electoral successes. Three locals in different areas ran their first candidates for office, and while the Burlington Greens of Vermont made a good showing, the Orange County Greens of North Carolina and the Lake Superior Greens of Wisconsin won seats on their county governing bodies.

In Maine the infighting of party- versus movement-types finally settled down, largely because those on the extreme ends of the debate had left. Those remaining turned to building local groups, one of which decided to shoot for a seat in the Maine legislature. Candidate Greg Gerritt, running as an independent because the party had not yet qualified for a ballot line, won an impressive 18% of the vote in a three-way race against the Democratic and Republican candidates. And a group in mid-coastal Maine won a fight against a waste incineration plant by campaigning in the name of Green values. A little over two years since their initial meeting, the mixed vision of a party within a movement seemed to be unfolding.

Out on the west coast the North California Greens became the regional umbrella for a host of active locals. The San Francisco Greens created working groups for issues such as toxic chemical use, community-based economics, and opposition to the forced relocation of 10,000 Navajo. The Sonoma

Greens planned a forum on wastewater treatment. The Mendocino Greens worked to ban offshore oil drilling and create a marine sanctuary, stop aerial spraying of pesticides, and improve drinking water quality. The East Bay Green Alliance sponsored public forums on environmental and economic topics. And the Central Coast Greens, established in January '86 for the Monterey area, brought together a coalition to fight the release of a genetically engineered microorganism on agricultural crops, the first proposal of its kind in history.

There were also Green locals active in Southern California from San Diego to Santa Barbara. In the Midwest there were the Prairie Region Greens and its most active local, the Kansas City Green Presence, as well as groups in St. Louis and Chicago. And in the Northwest there were groups in Eugene and Portland in Oregon and Seattle, Bellingham, Tacoma, Olympia and Whidbey Island in Washington State.

Despite the growth in grassroots activity and apparent resolution of the Clearing House issue, the disputes within the IC had not transformed into hand-holding harmony. On the first day of the March 1986 IC meeting in Seattle, before many of the delegates had arrived and with the participation of some non-delegates, a decision was made to bar two Wisconsin Greens who had been active in the Yippies and the socialist Labor-Farm Party from being observers at the meeting. When the other delegates arrived and learned of the pre-emptive decision, they raised questions about who had a right to participate in the CoC and in IC deliberations. A process for accrediting regional groups had not been created, and the consensus rule made it difficult to decide anything about it. (The rule was to seek consensus and use an 80% majority vote as a backup if needed, but reaching 80% was not much easier than reaching full consensus.) Spretnak laid out her view of the debate in the paperback edition of *Green Politics*, published later that summer:

Some Green groups or individuals, however, have issued

statements that are more leftist than Green, and while no one organization owns the entire American Green phenomenon, many American Greens feel that those groups, in deference to accuracy, should identify their operations as "leftist Green" rather than simply "Green." A more disturbing problem is that a few small groups using the name "Green" have employed aggressive and disruptive tactics to further their organizations and have issued material that is an embarrassment to the majority of American Greens. For example, at the March 1986 meeting of CoC's interregional committee a lengthy discussion was held on the need to clearly dissociate the Committees of Correspondence from any connection with "the Yippies, the Yippie Greens, the North American Green Network, the North American Green Communications Project, Green Census, the 'New York Greens,' the publication *Overthrow*, and all other Yippie front groups and publications."

The Youth International Party—or Yippies, a play on the word 'hippies'—was a loosely organized anarchist group that came out of the anti-war movement of the '60s and was known for politically-oriented public pranks and stunts. The social ecologists of the ISE, who also held anarchist views, interpreted Spretnak's remarks as another attempt to contain their influence, as Satin had tried to do at the founding meeting. They began to see Spretnak and the California Greens, in particular, as more concerned with the rights of nature than the rights of human beings, due to their friendliness to "deep ecology" philosophy and antipathy to socialism. Murray Bookchin and others who felt tagged by her "leftist Green" label spoke out against that position, often vehemently. For them a central issue was that the oppression of humans by humans was prior to the oppression of nature by humans, not vice versa.

The leading proponents of the rights of nature were not even a part of the CoC, but Spretnak had published *The Spiritual Dimension of Green Poli-*

tics in 1986, arguing for a common ground between ecofeminism and deep ecology in an earth-based spirituality. She and other ecofeminists critiqued the idea of a value-free pure rationalism, calling for recognition of traditionally "feminine" traits such as values and emotion in understanding the world and making decisions. CoC members like David Haenke, Dee Berry and John Rensenbrink were sympathetic to this viewpoint, drawing them together in common opposition to Bookchin's influence. They regarded the polemical style of debate he used as an aspect of patriarchy with its emphasis on dominating, and they wanted to counter this by seeking balance among the diverse viewpoints in the CoC. This was to their minds a more ecological perspective mirroring the dynamic balancing of the needs of different species in nature.

Tensions within the IC built during the lead-up to a planned second national meeting, which was set for July 1987 at Hampshire College in Amherst, Massachusetts. Controversy over decision-making rules for the meeting and whether/how to credential participants to vote at it resulted in an agreement to make it a purely educational event, aimed at airing the various differences of opinion within the CoC. The Northeast region, seen by many as a stronghold of what was now commonly coming to be referred to as the "left wing" of the Greens—primarily but not exclusively the social ecologists—was responsible for planning the events to fill the five days of the conference.

According to Howie Hawkins, the regional coordinator in the Northeast at the time and a committed democratic socialist, Spretnak saw the conference as being taken over by the left wing and turned down an invitation to be on a panel, refusing to attend and discouraging others from attending. But as the pre-registration numbers climbed she apparently changed her mind, insisting not only on joining an already-planned panel of speakers but on adding a dozen new workshops led by "spiritually oriented Greens" (Hawkins' words). The organizers acceded to her untimely requests in order to insure all views were given a hearing.

Now referred to as the first national U.S. Green "gathering," the conference was titled "Building the Green Movement: A National Conference for a New Politics." The brochure for the event stated:

> We invite all Greens and activists in kindred social change movements to participate in this educational conference. We are not gathering to make decisions for the Green movement. Our purpose is education. It will be a chance for Greens and activists in kindred movements from across the land to meet, share perspectives, and learn from each other—and take what we learn back to our communities to put into practice.

The diverse topics of the ten panels and 120 workshops included "Green Movements Around the World," "The Greens and Electoral Politics," "Green Economic Alternatives," "The Greens and the Labor Movement," and "Eco-Feminism and Spiritual Renewal." Over 600 people from thirty-eight states and nine countries officially attended, described by Satin as "a rather inauspicious-looking crew, clad as they mostly were in tank tops, T-shirts and blue jeans." Most participants were from the Northeast, but substantial numbers came from California and Wisconsin, with at least a few from nearly every state: "Farmers from Maine. Doctors from Virginia. Steel workers from Ohio. Comedians from California. Old beatniks and college newspaper editors. Trained technicians and Goddess worshippers."

An attempt to start off by cultivating a peaceful mindset misfired. A meditation session was held and although many attendees participated, others looked askance at this. Murray Bookchin, described by Satin as the "stocky, garrulous veteran of the communist and anarchist movements of the 1930s," was one of the latter. He gave a plenary address taking shots at the "spiritual" wing of the Greens and other perceived infidels, questioning whether rational thought was being abandoned in claims of transforming consciousness. He challenged his listeners as to whether they were a social movement or a religious one. Environmental issues couldn't be separated from social ones, he argued, again attacking deep ecologists for putting nature above human beings. If a plenary address is meant to set the themes of a conference, Bookchin's speech was a rousing success—and it roused a lot of people.

Spretnak's retort came in her address, posing the question of what a "politically correct" society would be like if it didn't address the needs of the heart and the soul. Social problems, in her view, were rooted in spiritual ones. Bookchin's daughter Debbie volleyed back at an open mike session, querying whether a spiritual perspective meant settling for reforming the market rather than overthrowing capitalism. Socialism had its own problems, David Haenke countered, so the goal should be reshaping capitalism in line with Green values. Howie Hawkins joined the fray, opining that only those who were fundamentally opposed to capitalism should be part of the Green movement. He also contended that Greens shouldn't engage with the Democratic and Republican parties, provoking Gerald Goldfarb to argue that Green caucuses in those parties would be a good thing and that no one should dictate to other Greens what they should or shouldn't do. Disputes could get heated, with some of Bookchin's followers even hurling epithets like "fascist" at Spretnak.

The dividing lines were not always clear. When Jutta Ditfurth of the West German Greens complained of "mysticism" pushing out rational political debate, Bookchin took the other side. He claimed that an ecological outlook could provide the spiritual meaning lacking in capitalist society, but he was concerned about the deep ecologists' spiritual elevation of nature. Spretnak, Rensenbrink, Dee Berry, and others took issue with his criticisms of deep ecology. Across the spectrum of views there was general agreement on the need to join politics and spirituality, with Rensenbrink quoting the Biblical exhortation to be as "wise as serpents and innocent as doves," but the precise role of spirituality was a topic bouncing like a ping pong ball from session to session.

The movement versus party split was also a hot topic, with the former side counseling that they should take the time to work out organizational practices based on Green values, while the latter expressed impatience to get on with it already. Ditfurth despaired that "nothing will *happen* after this conference," and Barbara Epstein, a professor of history and long-time activist, complained about the attachment to consensus decisions and the ideal of a leaderless organization. She cited a need for accountable democratic leadership in any serious and lasting organization. (As Mark Satin later reported, basic tasks like "fund raising, organizer training and membership building" had been neglected, noting that only eight people showed up for the workshop on fund raising.)

The negative and contentious spirit carried over into hallway grumbling about which speakers and topics were given time and which were left out or under-represented. Phrases like "rationalist patriarchy," "flaky spirituality," "strident Marxism," and "bourgeois bullshit" were overheard. Some sat through meditations and healing ceremonies "sullenly and resentfully" or pointedly walked out on them. Out of session gossip speculated about a feud between Bookchin and Spretnak or one side trying to drum the other out of the CoC. The central divide was as much about political style as political substance: confrontation and dialectical debate versus transcendence of old "isms" for the sake of healing and community building.

Not that the gathering was all stormy; shafts of sunlight did peek through here and there. Over "beans and rice on the picnic grounds, across the net on the campus tennis courts, and under the stars in nearby pastures," people shared inspiring stories about what their local and regional groups were doing. Garbage burning plants were being fought. Community gardens were planted in the ghetto. Local offices were being sought and won. Allegra Azouvi got a standing ovation for recommending people take some time out to just enjoy themselves at the gathering: "Give each other a massage, take naps." Attempts to find common ground were offered.

Finally a skilled mediator, Margot Adair of California, conducted a closed door session for Spretnak and Bookchin, with Berry and Rensenbrink invited to participate. They spent "three difficult hours" shut up in a room hashing out their differences. According to Hawkins, Spretnak blamed the problems on Bookchin and the other social ecologists while Bookchin suggested they put the past behind them and debate different views without personal attacks. After a kind of détente was attained, they appeared before the attendees at the final plenary session and gave each other a hug.

"We had a very sincere and deep reconciliation this afternoon," Spretnak said. "And the only reason we're giving you this dog-and-pony show here is to show you that if we can do it here, you can do it in your locals and regionals."

"I am still a leftist," Bookchin chimed in. "I am still a revolutionary. What Charlene and I have agreed to is to treat each other respectfully" in their debates. He added that he was still committed to promoting his political views within the organization.

As recounted by Hawkins, the "right wing was outraged at Bookchin's statement and in the next few years they would try to drive the left out of the Greens." His use of the phrase "right wing" indicates how polarized the movement was soon to become.

Rensenbrink, who at one of the closing sessions exhorted the attendees to rise above the perils of their movement to its promise, reported the aftermath of the gathering differently. The "attacks from Murray and his followers continued," he wrote. "This left a bitter residue and led to Charlene's withdrawal from an active role in the national Green movement and in party building."

Hawkins and Rensenbrink were each writing in hindsight, surveying the field of the struggle for when the battle lines were first drawn.

Alan F. Zundel

CHAPTER FIVE

The Factions Formalize

The immediate results of the July 1987 gathering seemed positive. It brought media attention to the CoC and stimulated the continued growth of locals, which almost doubled again from the previous year, reaching 150 chapters. Conflicting views had been aired and leaders from different factions made public commitments to work together. But the inability of the CoC's governing structure to resolve the differing perspectives was to push things in a different direction.

In evaluation sessions at the end of the gathering there were requests for future national meetings to focus on creating a common Green program, something more action-oriented to add to the Ten Key Values in tying the movement together. A month later the IC met in Kansas City and had an extensive discussion of the idea, considering various topics that should be covered, including strategy. Rensenbrink suggested soliciting topics and working papers from the Green locals and calling the overall program "Strategy and Policy Approaches in Key Areas," or SPAKA. The IC ratified the proposal and established a working group to coordinate with the locals in preparation for another gathering to consider the results. Rensenbrink and Margot Adair agreed to be coordinators of the process.

Rensenbrink and Dee Berry, in her role as Clearing House coordinator, put out the call for topics and position papers from the locals as well as from interested organizations and individuals. Hundreds of responses flowed into the Clearing House. At the next IC meeting, held in Austin in January 1988, the working group divided these into eleven categories. Over the next year and a half Rensenbrink guided deliberations among the locals and other participants as 190 position papers were developed, keeping members informed through the *Green Letter*. The Merrymeeting Greens chapter in Maine was assigned the task of further sorting the papers and came up with nineteen categories: energy, forest and forestry, life forms, material use and waste management, water/air, general economic analysis, finance, land use, politics, social justice, eco-philosophy, spirituality, education, food and agriculture, health, peace and nonviolence, community, organizing, and strategy. "Strategy" was included in anticipation that this might eventually become a platform for a political party. In California Jon Li condensed the 600 pages into forty-three, and activists in the PeaceNet/EcoNet computer network uploaded the summary and most of the papers for members' ease of access before the planned national gathering in summer 1989.

The 1989 gathering was to be a working meeting, not another educational event, with each local limited in the number of delegates they could send. It was also thought of as a practice session for making decisions together, with the SPAKA papers approved provisionally before final decisions to be made at a subsequent gathering. In Rensenbrink's eyes the year and a half preparatory process had privileged the lived experience of people at the grassroots, as was intended, instead of the usual reliance on the views of supposed experts. As the coordinators put it, "Democracy is not about deciding if you support this or that person to do politics for you. True democracy is creating policy collectively."

Howie Hawkins, who had agreed to the SPAKA decision at the August 1987 IC meeting in Kansas City, had other feelings. A few years later he wrote that when the IC consented to the proposal for developing SPAKA, they assumed the proposal would be sent to locals for discussion and modification before adoption. In his words:

> But instead it was sent by Rensenbrink to the CoC's national publication, *Green Letter*, as a final decision. Thus, without any grassroots debate, program writing, in addition to fighting over structure, became the preoccupation at the national level. The style in which this decision was made came to characterize the functioning of the right wing of the Greens over the next few years.

Hawkins was viewing things from his position as a leader of the left wing of the Greens. As recounted in the previous chapter, social ecologists and their allies within the CoC had come to be referred to as "leftists" or the "left wing," due as much to their militant style of arguing as to their explicitly socialist views. The sense of being attacked led the "left wing" to see those with differing views as being on the "right," at best politically errant and at worst defenders of the existing order. To an outside observer the label might be perplexing, as in the conventional political vocabulary the vast majority of the Greens, if not all of them, would be clearly on the left end of the political spectrum. But within the CoC the distinction became freighted with significance.

Born in 1952 and raised in a multi-racial neighborhood outside of San Francisco, Hawkins participated in the civil rights, anti-war, and environmental movements as a teenager and gathered signatures to put the Peace and Freedom Party on the California ballot. While attending Dartmouth College in Massachusetts he joined the Socialist Party USA, a faction of the old Socialist Party which reconstituted itself as a new incarnation of the party. Hawkins remained in the Northeast after leaving college for financial reasons. He worked as a carpenter while continuing his activism, and in the late '70s formed a construction cooperative specializing in energy efficiency and renewable energy. He worked on several election campaigns in the years preceding the founding of the CoC, including Bernie Sanders' early campaigns with the Liberty Union Party in Vermont and the Presidential campaigns of the Peace and Freedom Party in 1968, the People's Party in 1972, and the Citizens Party in 1980.

Hawkins came out of the latter experiences with a conviction that alternative parties should build local organizations and influence municipal politics rather than trying to grow a party from the top down via a Presidential campaign. He brought this and his socialist convictions into the CoC when he joined as one of the founders at the St. Paul convention, aligning him with Bookchin's social ecologists. Hawkins also took the position that representatives to the Greens' state, regional and national bodies should be held to clear mandates and recallable if they failed to accurately represent the views of their locals. In his view the "right wing of the Greens" advocated centralized decision making to the detriment of accountability to the grassroots membership.

Rensenbrink and Hawkins were not only both representatives on the IC, they also both lived in the Northeast, making them members of the same regional organization. Hawkins claimed that the NECoC during the time period from late 1987 became an arena for attacks on the left wing, cudgeling them with rumors, red-baiting and personal attacks. Meetings became "uncomfortable" and "unpleasant." They tried to offer their own program and action proposals including creating more functional organizational structures, but were hindered by the consensus-or-80%-majority rule. Since they preferred local action anyway, many simply stopped attending the regional meetings.

Meanwhile the social ecology versus deep ecology debate raged on in environmental journals, causing Murray Bookchin to call for a left wing caucus to be formed within the CoC to champion his position. Leftist Greens in the Northeast took up this idea after yet another of the "miserable" NECoC meetings in which they felt under fire. Some of them from Vermont and New Hampshire got together and formed a "Green Alliance" to articulate how their views on theory, strategy and internal process differed from what they disdainfully termed New Age Greens. They revised the Ten Key Values into twenty-one principles sorted into four categories: values, goals, strategies, and organization. At the heart of their revisions was a focus on social justice and anti-capitalism, born of their desire to link the Green movement to the Old and New Left which they believed had paved the way for it. They intended to inject the SPAKA process with more historical and analytical clarity and counter notions that changes in personal consciousness and lifestyle could be sufficient to meet the ecological crisis.

The Green Alliance put out a call, signed by about twenty-five people, which circulated with their accompanying principles among the like-minded around the country. Out of this discussion a Left Green Network (LGN) emerged to advance, within the CoC, its priorities:

- Social ecology: Greens should address the social justice issues underlying environmental problems,

- Anti-capitalism: Greens should advocate decentralized democratic socialism,

- Independent politics: Greens should align with neither of the dominant political parties,

- Majority rule with dissent: CoC policies should be determined by simple majority rule and minorities should have the right to stand aside or dissent but not to block decisions, and

- Confederal municipalism: Greens should build local citizen assemblies and municipal coalitions rather than working for reforms within state structures.

Hawkins was one of the founders of the LGN and began traveling the country to talk about their concerns. At the Austin IC meeting in January 1988, he told Rensenbrink that the purpose of the LGN was to "'Green' the left and to 'left' the Greens." At first Rensenbrink saw this as a plus, a way to raise awareness of social and economic issues among Greens more focused on the environment. Later he changed his mind, charging the LGN with doing more to "remake the Greens into a Left fringe sect than on any greening of the Left."

Other Greens came to resent the LGN insistence that Greens should be anti-capitalist as a "litmus test" to judge whether they were truly Green. Rensenbrink defended the non-LGN leadership as neither pro-capitalist nor anti-capitalist, rather they wanted to transcend old ideological categories and encompass diverse viewpoints within the framework of the Ten Key Values. But eventually, he writes, "We got angry at what seemed the mistreatment and bullying of people who didn't go 100 percent with a supposed correct line."

The alienation between the leftist Greens and those they perceived as right wing deepened. The LGN went on the offensive with articles in the *IC Bulletin* published through the Clearing House, along with issuing "commentary, criticisms and manifestos" which Rensenbrink characterized as "increasingly strident and sectarian." Many of their attacks were leveled at the IC and its lack of clear organizational rules and accountability. Hawkins began submitting various drafts of detailed bylaws to the IC in line with the LGN's position that the IC and regional organizations were too loosely structured and subject to minority obstruction. The NECoC meeting held in Boston in September 1988 had structural reform on the agenda, but due to these tensions only twenty-five people showed up and the situation was not resolved. It became the final meeting of the NECoC.

Over on the West Coast Bookchin's continued polemics targeting Spretnak and other California Greens created a "furor," especially among women. Many saw his attacks as being personal, stirring a potful of "hurt, anger, and frustration" that began to boil over. In the fall of 1988 several Northern California Greens put out a statement challenging what they regarded as falsehoods by leftists, such as that the debate over deep ecology was a major issue among Greens or that overthrowing capitalism was an accurate expression of their collective aims. Spretnak and Danny Moses authored an additional essay, appearing in early 1989, designed to correct leftist misrepresentations of other Greens as apolitical, uninterested in reaching out to people of color, being inadequately ecofeminist, or otherwise falling short of Green values.

In contrast to the division within the Northeast regional, the California Greens were busy with regional development. On September 30th to October 2nd of 1988 the Northern California Greens hosted a five day conference, "Greening the West," at a YMCA camp in a San Mateo County redwood grove near La Honda, just south of San Francisco. Spretnak was one of several speakers addressing the attendees, who numbered over 1,000—more than had officially attended the 1987 national Green gathering. One hundred and fifty of them participated in a workshop entitled "Towards a Green Party of the West: Local and Regional Electoral Strategies." From this came a support network, the Green Party of the West, for those Greens interested in pursuing electoral politics. The initiative for developing a party via a regional network for electoral work was destined to clash with the LGN's preference for "confederal municipalism."

The second Green gathering was scheduled to be held June 21st-25th 1989 in Eugene, Oregon, with discussion of SPAKA the main order of business. At a meeting in New Orleans that February the IC worked on a plan to allow time for all of the SPAKA papers to be considered and discussed. Seeking to balance participation and efficiency and to model the kind of social process they hoped to see in the larger world, they decided to use skilled facilitators to both ensure all voices were included and keep the process moving toward greater agreement. The hope was to avoid the kind of divisiveness that nearly disrupted the 1987 gathering, which at that point seemed a real threat.

Two months later, in Ames, Iowa, the LGN held its first national conference to do its own preparation for the gathering. By now the twenty-one principles issued by the Green Alliance had been edited into fourteen, which were adopted by the fifty or sixty people in attendance. They also ratified bylaws, made plans for a publication (which became *Left Green Notes*), set up governing structures, and committed to a handful of action projects. Their plan for the Eugene gathering was two-fold: to hold caucuses for discussion and education on their positions, and to insure that their voice was heard in the working groups for SPAKA.

As news of this further consolidation of the left spread, the reaction was immediate. Lorna Salzman wrote an article with the provocative title, "Is the Left Green Network Really Green?" Salzman rejected the LGN's fundamental premise, blaming environmental problems not on capitalism but on industrialism. She claimed that the LGN started from an economic analysis instead of an ecological one, in effect importing its own agenda into an organization which did not share it. Her article appeared in the very month that the Green gathering convened to determine that agenda. The outcome, however, was to be determined by the rank and file Greens who showed up, not the minority active in the ongoing debates.

The Eugene gathering was held on the pine-covered grounds of the University of Oregon, where more than 300 people, about 250 of whom were delegates, converged from over 200 locals. There was now at least one local chapter in almost every state, with most attendees coming from California and the Northeast, but Wisconsin, Texas, Colorado, Missouri, Kansas, Washington, D.C., and of course Oregon were well represented. Observers from friendly organizations and Green party representatives from Canada, Latin America and Western Europe were also present.

Recent news reports fueled heightened commitment to the cause. Massive oil spills in the Gulf of Mexico, Delaware Bay and Rhode Island Sound demonstrated the urgent need for a Green political movement, while electoral successes in Europe and the U.S. stoked optimism for the future. Greens had increased their representation in the European Parliament and now held national offices in nine nations: West Germany, Belgium, Luxemburg, Austria, Switzerland, Finland, Sweden, Italy and Portugal. In the U.S., twenty-five Greens had run for local office between 1985 and 1989 and seven of them won, among them a black city councilor in New Haven who helped break the stereotypical palette of uniformly white Greens. The mood was one of determination, a common desire for the Greens to build on their successes and move forward.

Including Mark Satin and Howie Hawkins, only five Greens who were at the first two national assemblies were at this one, reflecting the continued attrition of the founding members. Satin reported that the average age of Eugene attendees was just over 40, with fewer than 10% under 30. Two out of every seven were unmarried, a fact perhaps connected to the relatively low median household income of $25,000 despite the fact that two-thirds had some graduate education. (The national average for people with five years of college was more than twice that.) Satin concluded that these middle-aged, highly educated financial underperformers had been "deeply influenced by the idealistic values of the Sixties," but "wounded by them too."

Whether due to wounds or honest differences, the contention within the leadership surfaced at the outset of the gathering during a "mini" IC meeting that exhibited its characteristic "storminess and lack of clarity." The representatives spent hours debating structure and by-laws, only to leave with differing opinions as to what if anything had been agreed to. They also needed to replace Dee Berry as the Clearing House coordinator, as she had resigned from that position the previous year. The two finalist candidates were men who were suddenly passed over the next day for Mindy Lorenz, who insisted on a full-time salary and moving the Clearing House to Eugene. This with minimal IC discussion of such relevant issues as how they could afford to pay Lorenz (Berry had received a small monthly stipend of about $200 and warned that the Clearing House was running out of money), what Lorenz's priorities were, or whether it was a good idea to move the Clearing House. Yet contrary to what might be expected, this did not turn out to be a warmup for an equally acrimonious gathering.

The gathering itself kicked off with solstice rituals and speeches to a couple hundred people sprawled out "along the lawn, on the steps, under the trees" of the campus. Rensenbrink called for the Greens to move from a politics of protest toward working to build a political party, while Charlie Betz, a member of both the Youth Greens and the LGN, argued for an anti-capitalist "oppositional" politics. (The Youth Greens had formed during the previous year, inspired by Bookchin's social ecology and allied with the LGN.) Other speakers spoke for "love and understanding" or quoted musician Bob Marley, "Won't you help to sing/these songs of freedom!" A smorgasbord of perspectives to suit any Green's tastes.

The first two days were devoted to working groups for developing the SPAKA position papers into statements of philosophy and practical recommendations in each issue area. Fifty to sixty opinionated people attended the Thursday and Friday strategy workshop sessions, and about the only areas of wide agreement were that local organizing and community building were still important. Beyond that, there were multiple competing priorities. Satin wrote that so many points of view were fielded that:

> No one could have figured out what was really being said in the room—no one could have picked up on all the subtle thrusts and parries (New Left versus New Age, anarchists versus socialists, etc.) without having spent at least three years in the alternative political wars. An IQ of 130 of more would have helped, too.

One issue percolating through the strategy workshop sessions—as well as the politics workshop sessions—was whether the Greens should start focusing on national politics in addition to local. Mixed into this debate was the growing interest in creating state Green parties, as the idea of working within the Democratic Party had waned, unless via a possible alignment with the Rainbow Coalition. Dee Berry made the case for "multi-level movement building," backed by a representative of the Canadian Green Party who said their campaign for national parliamentary seats had a real impact on attention to environmental issues. Supporters of this position saw the need for more electoral coordination and shared learning across localities, which could best be organized nationally. Opponents feared resources would be strained by an expanded focus and essential work at the local level neglected, or argued that higher levels of government were inevitably less accountable and thus electoral participation in them was to be avoided as corrupting.

Some pro-elections people talked ambitiously of the Greens playing a role in the 1992 or 1996 Presidential campaigns, perhaps even a Green Party USA convention. Hawkins remembered the topic as being raised specifically by Rensenbrink and supported by only "a few liberals who had wandered in from the Rainbow Coalition and the Democratic Socialists of America." Rensenbrink contends that he was trying to provoke new ways of thinking about a national party and Presidential campaigns, such as a "community-presidency" in which candidates for President and Vice-President would run with their proposed cabinet members.

Although Rensenbrink felt there was attentive listening that brought people closer despite their differences, the strategy workshops hadn't reached any consensus before the clock ran out. They decided to break into voluntary mini-working groups to continue the discussions, which of course advantaged those most willing to sit through more meetings and discussions, a common problem for groups dedicated to grassroots democracy.

In the evenings the LGN held its planned caucuses, hosted by the nine or so of its members and allies from the Youth Greens who were present at the gathering. Satin described these as lively affairs that went on well past midnight, the arguing stretching on "interminably," the words "cascading out, on and on, endlessly." The organizers had expected ten to fifteen people to show up but attracted eighty or more at a time. In addition to the familiar social ecology contingent, Satin counted "social democrats, independent decentralists, academics, battle-scarred leftists (primarily refugees from one or more Marxist sects), and left youth"—not to mention the "post-leftists" there to question and challenge them. The leftists did not back down. They insisted they were not there just to capture the Greens for the left, as they were as frustrated with the traditional left as they were with the New Age Greens. Much of the pent-up passion from before the gathering was released through these "hot and heavy" LGN caucus debates—although heavier on the theoretical than the practical. But Hawkins saw the sessions as a success for helping dispel "the myths about the Left Greens that had been generated by the rumor mill."

The passion predictably spilled over into the SPAKA economics workshop. Most the leftists argued that capitalism was the driving force behind the industrial economy that was tearing up the eco-system, making an explicitly anti-capitalist position imperative to adopt. Others saw industrialism as a feature of both capitalist and socialist economies in the modern world and proposed a decentralized economy with a variety of enterprise models. To them the goal should be empowering people and their communities, not simply redistribution. Concern that an anti-capitalist position would alienate potential supporters was also expressed. Ultimately the workshop produced two economics statements, one leaning more socialist and the other more "entrepreneurial," but they found common ground in deploring "addictive consumerism" and "perpetual growth" while lauding "simpler, self-reliant lifestyles" as well as "an equitable distribution of basic goods and services."

The spiritual versus political debate which had sucked up so much energy at the first gathering, however, had subsided. Neither Spretnak nor Bookchin were present at the Eugene meeting, and the aging Bookchin was to pull back from active political work within a few years. Rensenbrink summed up the consensus of those present: "As a movement we need two legs to walk on. One is political and the other spiritual. Without either, we stumble. I think this conference shows we're ready to move."

Some late night changes to the weekend schedule were made on Friday evening to accommodate the need for more deliberation before decisions were attempted. On Saturday working groups were limited to giving reports and receiving feedback, leaving more discussion time before decisions to be made on Sunday. The Saturday session was a talky and sometimes boring process until suddenly interrupted by a gaggle of long-haired teens parading in with a giant replica reefer, chanting on behalf of marijuana legalization. Surprise, anger and embarrassed recognition of their younger selves helped to perk up the aging ex-hippies in the room. Fortunately someone invited the novice protestors to speak to the veteran protestors and all ended well. That night the Eugene local, which had been publishing a "*Green Tidings*" daily report on workshop developments, printed up the SPAKA statements as revised after feedback to disseminate to the attendees for the next day.

Finally, on the last day of the gathering, the statements were presented for the assembly's approval. They drew broad support (passing by consensus or at least a straw vote of 80%), with the LGN leaders satisfied that they had had significant input. The statements were adopted provisionally and passed on to the newsletter editors for publicizing and the working groups for further consideration. The end results were to be considered at the next national gathering, scheduled for the following year in Colorado. Ultimate decision making power at the next gathering was to be given to a new representative Assembly, made up of delegates from dues-paying locals and regionals. The attendees also added "Green" to the organization's name, becoming the Green Committees of Correspondence (GCoC) in belated acknowledgement of their European forebears. They closed with a picnic celebration in which "a hot, hot, hot Latin percussion band inspired a conga line" and jugs of "homemade brew" were passed around. As one observer noted in relief, "the gathering went more smoothly than anyone dared hope."

Sixty attendees stuck around for three long evaluation sessions afterward. They identified areas for improvement in future gatherings, but overall the week was deemed a success. The consensus process worked well due to good facilitators and careful planning, and the inclusion of activities such as hikes in the mountains, concerts, street fairs and forest projects afforded time to relax and recharge oneself. As Danny Moses of the Bay Area Greens commented:

> There's been the achievement of a kind of psychological soli-darity; a feeling of bonding with each other in a way that is critical to the work we want to do together. The Green movement is more present now, because of this…
>
> The feeling takes me back to the times I cherish and the work we did in the early 60s in the civil rights movement, which was an 'inspirited' movement—one in which spirit and analysis worked hand in hand to produce great results.

After all the conflicts of the previous three years, renewed hope was the order of the day.

CHAPTER SIX

Full-Fledged Fights

The participants at the 1989 gathering had deflected proposals for building state electoral parties, as many, particularly leftist Greens, were opposed to the idea. Yet efforts toward this end were taking place under their noses. Predictably, the Californians were the culprits. About fifty Greens from across California met in their first state caucus during the gathering and found that the presumed north/south divide in the state was not the barrier between them some had imagined it to be. Discussions about creating a state party had been initiated at the Greens of the West conference in Northern California the previous year, which had also produced the Green Party of the West support network for electoral work. The California caucus was encouraged enough to set up a working group to plan a statewide meeting for the fall.

The first meeting of the new statewide California Green Assembly took place in November at Cal State Fresno, with about twenty-five Greens from the three California GCoC regionals attending. They spent the day considering which issues California Greens might coalesce around, and then in the evening they turned to the topic of creating a state party. Opinion was mixed over whether to do this, and if so, how soon. They also became aware of a knotty problem. A small group called "Green Futures" had already obtained the right to create a Green Party in California, although they had fallen far short of getting the number of voter registrations needed. The two year window to accomplish this was to expire at the end of the year, but any attempt to pick up the name after them would inevitably cause confusion in the general public. On top of this, the California Democrats were backing a "Big Green" environmental ballot initiative, further complicating political use of the word "Green." Despite these complications the group chose two of its members to go to the state capitol and talk to the head of the Elections Division about securing the rights to the name. Those members would then report back to the California locals and a decision would be scheduled for a larger meeting in February.

On January 2nd, 1990, the two delegates filed to create a Green Party of California. They would need about 79,000 voter registrations (1% of the total number of votes cast for governor at the last election) within two years to qualify for the ballot. The Green Assembly met on February 4th at Cal State Sacramento, with Mike Feinstein and Mindy Lorenz as co-facilitators and sixty-five delegates and observers in attendance. There was general approval for having gained the right to the Green Party name but still disagreement about whether they were ready to follow through on creating a party. In the end they voted to move forward and established the Green Party of California, with twenty-seven locals in favor, three stand-asides, and no opposition. They also created committees to draft a platform and by-laws, designated Lorenz, Danny Moses and Dan Tarr as press contacts, and approved a pro bono state lobbyist. Lorenz and Kent Smith appeared on the television news that evening to announce the new party. On March 2nd the California Secretary of State approved the filing. Voters had begun registering with the party right after the name was filed, but now they had a green light to launch a large scale registration drive.

Similar plans were afoot in other states. In Michigan the Huron Valley Greens had a Working Group on Electoral Action which helped get a state party initiated in 1989. By January 1990 they had a platform and by-laws in place and the Working Group became a party chapter. The parent group, the Huron Valley Greens, remained a local of the Mid-Great Lakes Regional of the GCoC. This was a way of finessing the relationship between the new state party organization and state party chapters on one side, and the Mid-Great Lakes Regional and the Michigan GCoC locals on the other. The state party and the GCoC regional were thought of as "cooperating organizations" that would meet at the same time. A comparable relationship was created in California between the Green Party of California and the California Green Assembly of the GCoC.

Over in Maine, where the Greens had initially been organized as a state "party/movement," the state organization had fallen dormant while members worked on developing the locals. But electoral work had been on their agenda from the start, and as mentioned earlier Maine was the first state in which a Green ran for a state legislative seat. When representatives of nine locals met in February 1990 for a statewide meeting to talk about near and long term strategies, one of their decisions was to set up a "'92 Committee" to meet in April and create an electoral plan. Shortly after this Nancy Allen, a prominent Hancock County Democrat who was also a member of the Maine Rainbow Coalition, left the Democrats to establish a county Green Party chapter. This grabbed media attention and inspired the Greens at the April meeting to lay plans to run a candidate for Governor that year. If their candidate could get 5% of the vote, the party would win official status and could then run candidates for state and local offices under the party label in 1992. Unfortunately the chosen candidate backed out and the party could not find an acceptable replacement.

The Politics Working Group of the 1989 gathering had recommended "Greens begin running candidates at the local level and only proceed to the state and then to the national level when there were a substantial number of Green officeholders at the level immediately below." Many wanted to speed up that process. At the October 1989 IC meeting in Washington, D.C., John Rensenbrink and Matt Tilley, the representatives from Maine, proposed a

Working Group on Electoral Action. Members of the LGN opposed this forcefully, suspecting it was born of opportunism on the part of "aspiring politicians" and would be a step toward accommodation with the political establishment. As at the national gathering four months earlier, there were also members who worried about this distracting from movement organizing at the local level. Despite these concerns and to Rensenbrink's surprise, the proposal passed with 91% in favor. The resistance to this development was obvious in the minutes for the meeting, which dwelt more on criticisms of the motion than arguments in favor.

What was gradually becoming clear to the proponents of state parties was that while they saw electoral work as one of many strategies the Greens should embrace, others saw that particular strategy as a threat to be squelched. At least part of the LGN's opposition was based on their preferred strategy of confederal municipalism. Others feared that all the focus and energy would get sucked into electoral work, leaving little for issue activism, public education, promoting lifestyle changes, or building alternative institutions. In addition, progressives and left-wingers inside and outside the Greens worked to hinder Green party building in favor of working within the Democratic Party, or organizing a labor, black, progressive or some other kind of party instead. The more the opponents of state Green parties resisted, the more the proponents turned to working outside the purview of the GCoC, which opponents found even more objectionable. Something had to give.

Within four months of its creation the Working Group on Electoral Action had ballooned in membership, and in a dramatic step before the March IC meeting in San Diego it separated from the GCoC and renamed itself the Green Party Organizing Committee (GPOC). The fifteen members present signed a unanimous statement which said, in part:

> The relationship of this new group to the IC and the Green Committees of Correspondence was discussed and the following points were

agreed upon: 1. That we consider ourselves a cooperating organization but autonomous from the IC and the GCOC; 2. We consider ourselves morally accountable to not only the Green Committees of Correspondence but the entire Green Movement.

When the decision was reported to the IC on the following day, the delegates applauded the move before voting to ratify a "cooperating organization" arrangement. Unhappy members of the LGN regrouped to counterattack at the June IC meeting in Ann Arbor, Michigan, but their demand that GPOC revert to a working group within the structure of the GCoC was refused.

Pushback was more successful in the states, at least at first. When the California Green Assembly met in Los Angeles in late March, some of those present accused the people promoting a state party of being an unrepresentative minority ignoring regular process. A shouting match broke out and Mindy Lorenz was physically assaulted, causing the pro-party people to abandon the meeting and regroup in Glendale. Still they managed to launch a registration drive on Earth Day, April 22nd, tabling at events across the state and doing especially well in San Diego, where they registered about a thousand voters. Although the California Green Assembly never met again, the state party people met in May to set up working groups, a Coordinating Committee, and provisional bylaws for a reconfigured organization. However, relations with GCoC locals were uneasy and the registration drive soon began to lag. The Michigan Green Party cooperating relationship with the Mid-Great Lakes Regional was also faltering.

In May Carl Boggs, an author active in local and state Green meetings in California, published an essay in the *Greens Bulletin* which raised the debate into the national Green consciousness. "Why the California Greens Should Wait to Have a Party" was a summary of the case against the current party activism. Boggs claimed the meetings of the statewide California Green Assembly were undemocratic due to lack of notification and low attendance, and those involved failed to give due consideration to arguments on both sides of the issue. The political experience of European Green parties or previous U.S. alternative parties hadn't been closely examined. The grassroots base of the party wasn't wide enough yet for supporting the type of coalition needed to have a realistic chance of winning offices above the local level. Credibility with other groups, such as labor or people of color, could be crippled, and with repeated electoral losses discouragement among Green supporters would set in. Pro-party Greens fired back, noting the increased public visibility of the California Greens since starting a party, the right of a group of individual Greens to initiate their own activities, and that the accountability of a state party would rightly be to party registrants rather than members of GCoC locals.

State party organizing was not the only area of conflict again cropping up. Immediately after the 1989 Eugene gathering, LGN members responded to Lorna Salzman's article criticizing them.[6] This provoked Spretnak to answer back on various points. But the exchange was set aside by the LGN as they became immersed in planning an Earth Day action for Wall Street meant to shift responsibility for environmental action from consumers to corporations. Greens at the gathering had responded well to the idea, but the LGN could not get consensus support from the IC when they tried in October or again the following March. At issue once more was the correct stance on capitalism. Although they had endorsements from over forty-five other organizations, the LGN proceeded without an endorsement from the GCoC, pulling off an environmental demonstration involving nearly two thousand people and gaining widespread media coverage. But it did nothing to pull the Greens together, instead leaving LGN members even more frustrated with the internal process of the GCoC.

Fund raising was another problem area, and had been from the start of

---

[6] As mentioned in the previous chapter, the article was published in the same month that the national gathering was held.

the CoC in 1984. Greens have often been ambivalent about money, associating most social ills with the pursuit of filthy lucre. Locals subsequently lagged in collecting money to pay their expected dues, and even by 1989 only forty locals had met their obligations. The idea of hiring staff to cultivate dues paying members became entangled with the sparring over the role of the Clearing House and never happened. Despite the clear need for it, attendance at the fund raising workshop in the 1987 gathering was sparse. And at the IC meeting a month after that gathering, a proposal to create a fund raising program under the non-profit rules of the national tax laws was dropped due to opposition from the delegates of two regions.

In 1988 a Fund-Raising Working Group finally got off the ground, thanks to the leadership of Sue Conti. Conti envisioned a well-funded education and development fund and began working with a highly regarded lawyer to structure it. But she ran into the pervasive distaste for facing money issues, the fears of centralized power that her proposal represented to some, and continual demands from the IC to revise one detail or another of her proposal. The tax lawyer struggled to align IC demands for grassroots accountability with tax law requirements, as most non-profits are structured with a clear executive authority responsible for decisions. Finally he gave up and sent a sizable bill for his unfinished work. The ill will that had built up between various people over the course of this debacle caused Conti to despair of accomplishing anything. In October of 1989, after relentless criticism of her efforts, she tearfully resigned and left the Greens, comparing her experience to enduring an abusive marriage. Over half the working group also left. In January the four remaining members started picking up the pieces, but the going had not become much easier despite the growing recognition throughout the GCoC that people needed to find a way to work together more cooperatively.

Christa Slaton, a political scientist and co-founder of the Green Party of Hawai'i who had recently moved to Alabama, was at that October meeting. She had just taken on the role of overseer of the SPAKA development process that day, succeeding John Rensenbrink, who remained involved as an advisor. Slaton later wrote that Conti's speech "hit me like a ton of bricks." The various working groups and caucuses at the Eugene gathering had appointed two people in each issue area to take responsibility for revising their piece of the SPAKA text, charged with working in collaboration with whichever working groups had an interest in the topic. Despite having the provisionally accepted SPAKA planks to work with, the process was complicated by the expanded number of people involved. As foreshadowed by Conti's ordeal, Slaton had trouble getting the volunteers to work together and meet deadlines. Arguments between members of working groups or between members of working groups and GCoC locals continually erupted. She found herself spending her time prodding, cajoling and mediating between people to just keep the process on track. She expected it to be hard work, but:

> The issue was how each step of progress constantly made had to be retraced as new people got involved and folks participated haphazardly at their own convenience. Time after time, decisions that were made through open group process were altered at the next meeting by a different group of decision-makers... [The Greens] act frantically, illogically and chaotically. They've had many experiences telling them it is foolhardy to trust, and, by George, they aren't trusting anybody.

The failure of two-thirds of the locals to pay their dues added to the problem, because it meant most GCoC members were not even receiving updates on the process from the *Green Letter*. The Planning Group for the upcoming September 1990 gathering, concerned about members coming to agreement for final decisions on SPAKA, recommended to the IC that the rule for a passing vote in case of lack of consensus be reduced from 80% to 75%. The group also recommended philosophical preambles be ignored in favor of practical recommendations, as agreement on political philosophy seemed to be the chief bone of contention. The IC approved these changes, and going into spring 1990 the process seemed to be working more smoothly. But trouble was brewing behind the scenes.

In May Howie Hawkins published an article about widespread dissatisfaction with the GCoC and how its dysfunctions led both party and movement activists to take action outside the formal structure. He proposed a "Greens for Democracy" group to advance structural reforms such as majority rule which he believed would allow the GCoC to bring the wings of the movement back together as a unified force. Hawkins, Charlie Betz, and Lauren Sargent of Michigan presented a restructuring proposal at the June IC meeting during which the complaints about GPOC independence were raised. Their request to dedicate a whole morning of the national gathering to making decisions on their proposal was resisted by the Planning Group on the grounds that such an important topic couldn't be addressed adequately within the limited time that could be taken from working on the SPAKA text. The result was a compromise allowing time at the gathering to discuss restructuring but postponing any decisions about it until a later date. They also formed a committee to prepare a proposal for the discussion.

The LGN held its second national meeting in Plainfield, Vermont, from June 30th to July 2nd, one month after the IC fights over the independence of GPOC and the restructuring proposal. About fifty people attended. The LGN experienced its own internal conflicts at the meeting which paralleled those that had ruffled the GCoC, primarily over Bookchin's dogmatic insistence on confederal municipalism and the issue of aggressive male argumentation. But they agreed on supporting Hawkins' Greens for Democracy proposal to reform the GCoC's structure and process.

Later in July the *Green Letter* was able to publish a full version of the SPAKA text to be considered at the gathering. Locals were notified that any critical responses had to be submitted by August 20th, and many of them began responding with careful critiques and alternative recommendations. Shortly after this Hawkins and Brian Tokar began distributing a letter throughout the GCoC using the Greens for Democracy name and attacking the prohibition on offering new material for SPAKA at the gathering as "undemocratic." They also blamed the dysfunctions of the IC on manipulation by behind-the-scenes cliques and revived the call for scheduling time at the gathering for restructuring decisions. Slaton responding by defending the SPAKA process in the *IC Bulletin*, pointing out that she repeatedly had asked the critics for input on the text over the preceding year but they hadn't responded, and that the August deadline for new material was agreed to when the process was set and was well publicized in advance.

Complaints were also popping up from other quarters. An active local in the Midwest wanted any SPAKA decisions at the gathering to be sent to all the GCoC members for ratification, despite the three years already spent on discussions in the locals. Some people protested that the $250 fee for the five-day gathering was too steep, even though the GCoC was still in debt from paying off the last two gatherings. As the various complaints seemed to originate from some of the same people, the Planning Group began worrying about a plot to sabotage the gathering.

A week before the gathering, Slaton, Rensenbrink and Margot Adair, who as an editor of the *Green Letter* was part of the Planning Group, met in San Francisco to reassess the plan for the SPAKA ratification process in case problems arose. They made a few changes to mollify critics, the most important of which accommodated the desire to introduce new material. The workshops on the various issue areas would first consider proposed changes to the text that had come through the established process, and then if at least a third of the members wanted to consider new material it would be allowed. A few days later, as delegates began arriving on the evening before the gathering, the team was gratified to find that even the leaders of Greens for Democracy accepted the workshop design. But the appearance of comity was an illusion soon to dissipate like a morning mist.

The gathering was held in Estes Park, Colorado in September 1990, at a

YMCA camp in the Rocky Mountains. Each local with at least three dues paying members was allowed to send one delegate, with locals having a higher number of dues paying members allowed progressively more delegates up to a ceiling of five. At the opening session Matthew Gilbert, the exhausted site coordinator, took to the podium intending to make some inspiring remarks. Instead, looking out at the 200 delegates, he sounded cautious: "Try to find the space inside of you that's calm… We may have differences of opinion, but let's remember, we are really all friends here." The next speaker, Christa Slaton—"an intense, wiry redhead," as Mark Satin described her—was beyond exhausted. She tried to give a pep talk but was battling other feelings as she looked out at the people who had been criticizing her the last several months. Coordinating the SPAKA process was "one of the most difficult things I've done in my life," she acknowledged, but she was kept going by all the "good souls" out there. To her critics, though, this was more of the same aggrieved self-martyrdom they were tired of.

Throughout Thursday the SPAKA workshops dutifully discussed their parts of the text, and after some adjustments in the process over the course of the day they were functioning smoothly and reaching agreements. As had happened at the previous gathering, the economics workshop became divided over the question of explicitly targeting capitalism. Hawkins drafted a more radically socialist alternative to the working group document which ultimately passed after a revision adding elements from the latter. However, the result was what the left regarded as merely a social democratic plank as it retained no mention of changing the capitalist system. Rensenbrink, in contrast, later characterized the plank as having a "knee-jerk anticapitalist and pro-socialist cast to it."

Meanwhile that evening, even as some of the workshops continued their revisions, a large group of Greens held a "marathon" unscheduled meeting to discuss the unresolved issue of restructuring the IC. They began debating whether the restructuring committee's proposal should be voted on that weekend. Dee Berry objected that the committee hadn't really represented the grassroots, at which point Lauren Sargent became impatient. "I'd hate for us to initiate another whole process now. Our organization is falling apart!" Some began arguing over who should be on any new committee, while others insisted on sending the proposal to the locals for discussion before any vote was taken. "If I described this process to any progressive group in the country," Nicholas Dykema interjected, "they'd laugh me out of the room." After several such fraught meetings over the next few days, the end result was the creation of a new restructuring committee—once again kicking the can down the road.

On Friday morning the time came to consider the fruits of all the labor on SPAKA. Some delegates insisted that before they could vote, they needed to know whether the revised text would be sent back to the entire member-ship for approval as had been repeatedly requested. After some dissension the facilitator managed to hold the group to the plan to take that issue up on Sunday. To address the tensions in the air Margot Adair led them in an im-promptu guided meditation. Then the platform planks were discussed one by one, the clock ticking all the while as people began advancing new criti-cisms of them. "All these objections could have been raised anytime in the last two years!" an exasperated attendee shouted. Most of the planks were failing to reach the 75% vote threshold and so would have to go back to the workshops for further revisions.

That afternoon the coordinating team for the gathering made a proposal to change the process. Considering that after the day's votes many of the workshops would need to continue their deliberations, instead of returning to another plenary session for approval the delegates could cast secret bal-lots throughout Saturday and into Sunday. That way weekend sessions on strategy and coalition building wouldn't need to be rescheduled. This pro-posal was accepted. Slaton also explained a proposal for the SPAKA text to then go back to the local chapters for a vote, with 75% of the locals' approval needed to ratify it. This was intended as a compromise with critics, but Lau-ren Sargent objected that the SPAKA text should go back to the individual members, not the chapters. Slaton began to lose her composure, complaining about how difficult it had been to get people to meet deadlines in the first place. This in turn riled her opponents, who began accusing the coordinating team of being irresponsible and hogging the microphone. Jeff Allen criticized Slaton for giving in to "violent emotions," and someone else said she was talking down to people. Slaton, her insides churning, began expressing her dismay at how her good mood had been dampened by this development and chided the group about appreciating those who had been working so hard to get this done. Emotions were escalating, the tensions of the last few years climaxing.

Mark Satin, among others who witnessed things unravelling, was reaching a point of disillusionment. As he later wrote:

> For *seven years* the Greens had been saying that they were moving so slow because they—unlike other political groups—were committed to treating their members as Human Beings...
>
> But sitting there watching Slaton and Sargent and the others, and remembering the vast cast of characters that had passed through the Greens over the years, never to return, I could no longer believe that the Greens had any kind of special handle on sensitivity to others.
>
> On the whole, I thought, they treated each other no better than people did in Common Cause or NARAL or the Democratic Party. And sometimes they treated each other much worse.

Ultimately Slaton could take no more and left the room in tears. The delegates, somewhat sobered by this, resumed their work. That night an upbeat keystone speech by Walter Bresette, an Ojibwa activist from Wisconsin, helped revive people's spirits, and by Saturday morning the SPAKA deliberations were finally finished. A celebratory mood had begun to take hold when John Rensenbrink suddenly announced that their success had come at a cost:

Christa Slaton left the Greens. He chastised people for bullying others, particularly women, and not even recognizing when they were doing it. As for him, he said he withdrawing from any further involvement in the program process and instead was going to direct his efforts toward electoral politics and a "national inter-movement and multi-cultural gathering," a coalition building idea that had been approved by the IC in June. He finished by saying, "I've enjoyed working with you," invited people to an ad hoc meeting outside to talk about electoral work, and walked out.

Shock and confusion filled the room as people tried to absorb the meaning of his words. Rensenbrink had become a widely recognized leader in the GCoC and his speech had shaken them. A facilitator said Rensenbrink had told him not to let people clap, but they could stand if they chose to. People stood and some began weeping. Others were uncomfortable standing there, feeling unfairly maligned by a one-sided diatribe. The facilitator suggested they bow in respect for Rensenbrink's service to the Greens over the last several years, but only half the room complied. The rest felt the facilitator was manipulating them into insincere gestures.

Although many mistakenly thought Rensenbrink had left the Greens when he walked out, he was there that evening when a group of about thirty met to discuss developing coalitions with people of color. (Only three or four of those present fit that description.) Nerves were still raw and this meeting also went off the rails. After opening remarks from Danny Moses and Native American Roberto Mendoza, Rensenbrink opined that their comments weren't "practical." This generated calls for a woman's perspective, so Irene Diamond, the editor of an anthology on ecofeminism, attempted conciliation. She said that Rensenbrink expressed a more "mainstream" view while Moses and Mendoza were drawing upon the wisdom of "grassroots women, peasant people and indigenous peoples," but that both were valid perspectives. Kwazi Nkrumah, a labor activist from California, took offense at this. He angrily defended Rensenbrink before storming out shouting "I am not a peasant people!" He warned someone who passed him in the hall to get out of his way before he hit somebody. Those left behind were at first stunned, and as the discussion resumed it began turning toward various perceived shortcomings within the Greens. Most of the comments, Satin reports, were "riddled with blame, anger, guilt and/or self-flagellation."

At the final session the next day, those who were left began finishing up business and appointing people to new working groups. All of the SPAKA planks had received the needed votes to pass and the delegates had accepted the proposal to send them to the locals for ratification. Before the session ended, Christa Slaton's husband took the stage to read a letter from her about her decisions to leave the Greens. It expressed "regret that my wounds are so deep" and exhorted people "to change the way we treat each other." Afterward Kwazi Nkrumah took the microphone to rage for nearly twenty minutes about the problems he saw. "I was angry last night because people who know better, still can't get rid of their garbage... We should not let Christa leave this movement! If you do let her, don't you dare come to me pretending to be my friend!"

On this depressing note, people departed with mixed feelings about the gathering. Once again some of them, this time including Mark Satin, never returned. Others determined to stick with it and work harder to advance the values that the Greens proclaimed. The problem remained, however, that they had different strategies in mind of how best to do this.

Alan F. Zundel

CHAPTER SEVEN

Facedown of Forces

Three working groups were created at the 1990 Estes Park gathering: one to work on stylistic improvements of the SPAKA text, one to generate a proposal for restructuring the GCoC, and one to plan the next national gathering, which was to make decisions on restructuring. There was no working group on state parties. Officially the GCoC maintained the 1989 Politics Working Group position that Greens should refrain from state and national electoral activity until they were well established in offices at the local level. Dissenters had turned to working within GPOC, where over time they became increasingly convinced that electoral politics needed to be given precedence as the best way to break out of a sectarian "in-group" mindset and reach out to the general public. They also saw state and national electoral campaigns as a particularly effective way to do this.

On the penultimate day of the Estes Park gathering, John Rensenbrink had assembled some fifty like-minded Greens out on the lawn for a couple of meetings to talk about electoral and party-building work in their respective states. They compiled membership lists for GPOC, planned a newsletter, and set a February date for GPOC to meet again. It had been meeting in conjunction with IC meetings, but now the status of the IC was in limbo while the Restructuring Working Group did its work. Regardless of the enthusiasm of the GPOC Greens, the future of state party building was at this point still a little hazy. To date no Green Party had gained official recognition as a party or a ballot line in any of the fifty states.

That, however, was soon to change—and in an unexpected location. The Alaskan Greens had an advantage in gathering voter signatures, as their state had the second smallest population of all the states, with about 40% of the population centered in one city, Anchorage. The Greens managed to get 2,035 petition signatures, passing the requisite 1% of the electorate required to get their candidates for governor and lieutenant governor on the November ballot. Unfortunately, they missed the August 1st filing deadline and state officials refused their petition. Jim Sykes, a co-founder of the Alaska Green Party and its gubernatorial candidate, brought a successful lawsuit against the state based on previous ballot access cases by the Alaskan Independence Party. The Green candidates got on the ballot and Sykes won 3.3% of the vote in the November 1990 election, passing the 3% threshold to become a recognized political party in Alaska.

This milestone was a news item around the nation and put wind in the GPOC sails. In addition, nine of the twenty-one Green candidates running for office across the nation won seats, six of them in California. As a comparison, recall that from their first races in 1985 up through 1989 only twenty-five Greens had run for office and seven had been elected. November 1990 was a decisive step forward in electoral work.

The California voter registration drive was still ongoing, given extra impetus by Mindy Lorenz in her write-in campaign for a Congressional seat, the first U.S. Green to run for a national office. (She received about 1% of the vote, high for a write-in candidate.) Yet still they had collected only about 13,000 voter registrations, less than 20% of those needed by the end of the following year. In early January a small group of Greens in the Bay area got together to plan a more focused registration drive, calling themselves the Q Group. The Green Party of California had scheduled a meeting in San Francisco later in the month, and the Q Group was kicking around ideas such as raising money to hire a professional organizer. Fate intervened in the form of the January 16th commencement of U.S. bombing of Iraqi targets, the start of the Gulf War. The party meeting took place right at the time of major street protests against the bombing, and the Greens stopped their meeting to join the protests and collect voter registrations at the same time. As the Democratic Congress had closed ranks behind President George H.W. Bush to authorize the bombing, the Greens found progressives and anti-war people not only open to the Greens but actively seeking them out. They collected 700 signatures in an hour and a half before returning to their meeting.

Meanwhile Rensenbrink and Lorenz worked the phones to plan for the GPOC meeting. GPOC members had been invited to choose one or two people per state—four in the case of California—to send to the meeting in order to keep it small. The aim was to become better organized. Twenty-four people met February 8th-9th in Boston and set up multiple committees: Steering, Fund Raising, Organizing (for outreach to contacts around the country), Platform/Publicity, and Liaison with Potential 1992 Presidential Candidates. The latter committee was formed due to interest in the plans of Ron Daniels of the Rainbow Coalition, who had worked on Jesse Jackson's 1984 and 1988 Presidential campaigns and was considering a run himself in '92. The GPOC people were intent on networking with the many organizations looking at building a progressive "Third Force" in national politics for the upcoming election year—not just the Rainbow Coalition, but women's, labor, environmental justice, people of color and other groups—and determined to send representatives to the Atlanta Green Justice Conference for Cultural Diversity and Progressive Movements planned for June. Motivation was high at the Boston GPOC meeting and the primary message to the participants was to go back to your states and get parties started.

They also discussed a set of proposals advanced by the GCoC Restructuring Working Group, which had met at the end of November. The proposals would change the name from the Green Committees of Correspondence to The Greens (usa), establish an annual gathering of delegates from each dues-paying local, create a seven-member Coordinating Committee to oversee working groups and the Clearing House, create a mediation committee to work out differences between members, and replace the IC with a more authoritative two-branch Green Council composed of a delegate from each of eleven regions in one branch and eleven delegates chosen from Green parties around the country in the other branch. The two branches would meet both separately and together. This bicameral feature, which aimed to bring GPOC back within the fold of the larger organization, generated some skepticism at the GPOC meeting, but with some persuasion from Dee Berry and Charlie Betz they endorsed it along with the other proposals. When they announced this in their new newsletter they made it clear that their endorsement did not imply a surrender of the ability to act with some degree of independence.

However, when the restructuring proposals went to the GCoC locals for a vote in April, LGN members came out in force against the bicameral idea. (There were about 350 LGN members by this point.) The Restructuring Working Group had been co-chaired by Dee Berry, an ally of Rensenbrink, and Charlie Betz of the LGN. Its members represented the diverse regions and wings of the GCoC, and they had labored to create a structure which would win broad support. But the LGN viewed the GPOC reservation of independent action as a rejection of accountability to the grassroots: "a small group of self-appointed 'leaders' whose party building efforts are for the most part based on bureaucratic empire building, not grassroots organizing." They were also incensed that Howie Hawkins and Guy Chichester had been refused admittance to the Boston GPOC meeting, although they were not GPOC members and had not been chosen to attend by the GPOC people in their regions. Hawkins and the LGN advanced a competing "unified structure" proposal meant to nullify any independence of a state party branch in the new structure. By attacking the bicameral proposal as a threat to Green unity, they won the support of some New Age Greens who wanted group harmony to overcome organizational conflict and favored lifestyle changes as a strategy over electoral politics. It did not help matters that many election-oriented Green locals, especially in California, had ceased paying dues to the GCoC and so did not participate in the vote. While the other proposals were overwhelmingly approved, the bicameral proposal failed by a narrow margin.

In light of this outcome, when the GPOC Steering Council met in Atlanta that June they decided that at their upcoming general membership meeting they would present a variety of restructuring proposals for their members to choose from for endorsement. The membership meeting was to be held just before the next GCoC national gathering in mid-August. The Steering Council proposals ranged from full integration of the two organizations to remaining separate while maintaining lines of communication with each other. The Steering Council also planned other ideas to present to their members, including shifting GPOC membership from individuals to state party organizations and inviting Ron Daniels to address them at their meeting.

Afterward Rensenbrink and other GPOC leaders worked to compose a more specific restructuring proposal. This one would have representatives from GPOC and the GCoC hold seats on each other's governing bodies, solve problems with a mediation board, and have a GCoC working group on electoral activities cooperate with GPOC on shared goals. They were trying to come up with a compromise proposal to head off an unpalatable result at the national gathering. GPOC could choose to ignore any new GCoC restructuring and maintain its independence, but it had overlapping membership with the parent organization and a complete sundering could cost it members or create an internal GPOC schism. There was also the danger that two organizations competing for members' allegiance could cripple the entire Green movement.

A month later the LGN held its third national conference in Chicago. They were to consider a draft of their own program, which many members were criticizing as more social democratic than socialist, but got hung up on arguments about whether to remain an independent organization—which they had been faulting GPOC for being—or merge into the GCoC as a caucus once a restructuring plan was adopted. Some had become more favorable toward the GCoC because they had been able to influence the SPAKA planks, while others were becoming disenchanted with the general direction of the LGN, especially with what they regarded as a downplaying of racial and sexual identity politics. In short, both GPOC and the LGN were wrestling with their prospective future in a newly reorganized GCoC.

Restructuring the GCoC had become an escalating issue due to longstanding frustrations on all sides with the dysfunctions of the IC. When the IC was set up at the 1984 founding meeting, it was deliberately designed to have limited powers so that strong local chapters could be cultivated in line with the principle of grassroots democracy. As a result, it was difficult to get the IC to act when decisions for the whole organization needed to be made. The consensus-seeking norm was often interpreted in such a way that any one member of the IC could "block" an action, leading to lengthy and contentious debates that seemed to go nowhere. Delegates to the IC were volunteers and travelling to meetings in distant locations was a strain on their time and finances, so participation was episodic at best and deteriorated as the meetings rarely seemed to resolve anything. This also meant a decision made at one meeting could be unmade at another because different people showed up. These liabilities were quickly recognized, but the same liabilities impeded attempts to create an improved structure. Tensions built over the years until restructuring became a necessity if the organization was to hold together, even though by this time the consensus-or-80% rule had already been changed to consensus-or-majority vote. Now the question of GPOC's position vis-à-vis the GCoC was at the center of the restructuring issue, despite the fact that the LGN also maintained organizational independence.

The fourth national Green gathering was scheduled for August 16th-

21st, 1991 in Elkins, West Virginia. The GPOC membership meeting was to convene two days before the gathering in the same location. That July Charlie Betz lit a fuse by circulating a fiery letter to the 300 or so Green locals around the country. Betz was both a member of the LGN and a participant in GPOC. He led in the formation of the bicameral proposal of the Restructuring Working Group and had attended the February GPOC meeting and the June GPOC Steering Council meeting. But by July his attitude had changed, presumably influenced by other members of the LGN such as Howie Hawkins. In Hawkins' eyes GPOC wanted "the GCoC's blessing to give it legitimacy" without being accountable to the GCoC or their membership. In a similar fashion, Betz's letter attacked GPOC leaders for wanting to separate from and maybe even replace the GCoC, warning local chapters of the "dangers" of this path and exhorting them to resist these machinations.

The fuse ignited a horde of concerned, angry, and confused Greens, who exploded into the August GPOC meeting, admitted by GPOC secretary Phil Rose. LGN members (according to Hawkins, only five of the sixty or more attendees), New Age Greens, and other opponents of the state party wing of the movement were among them. When GPOC leaders held an impromptu early morning meeting to figure out how to respond to the hijacking of their planned agenda, they were accused of elitism and back room plotting. In Hawkins' telling, the GPOC leaders accused the leftists of trying to take over and control the Greens with their own agenda. According to Rensenbrink, he and other GPOC leaders tried to calm and reassure people, arguing for a diversity of approaches to shared goals, or as Rensenbrink put it, a "House of Green" with many rooms. They also touched on what Rensenbrink later called the "ideological chasm" between the LGN's eco-anarchism and their own idea of transformative political action, but they downplayed the incompatibility between them so as not to further split the already divided movement.

After spending that Wednesday and most of Thursday in inconclusive arguing, someone recommended the "key players" get together and come up with a proposal that the group could consider early the next morning, before the opening of the GCoC gathering. This was quickly agreed to. Rensenbrink, Hawkins, Betz, Lorenz, Berry, Kwazi Nkrumah and another African-American, Suleiman Mahdi, who had hosted the GPOC Steering Council meeting in Atlanta, along with a few others, were present for the Thursday night session. Danny Moses facilitated. They spun their wheels at first re-hashing the same arguments, but during a break Lorenz persuaded some of them to a new compromise proposal. This would integrate GPOC within the larger organization, but give state party and issue activists separate access to a Joint Board. After a lengthy, difficult discussion, everyone signed on to it but Betz and Hawkins. Betz seemed to be wavering, and Valerie Ackerman from Michigan, who was not affiliated with either the "left" or "right" Greens, made a moving plea for them to focus on their real relationships to one another rather than the mental constructs often confused with principle. The room was quiet as she talked, and even Hawkins seemed to be relenting. Then he "squared his shoulders and said he could not." Betz went along with him.

Nkrumah and Mahdi then spoke regretfully of how at one time two factions of the black movement had almost overcome their differences and come together, but failed at the key moment and missed their chance, much to the detriment of the larger movement. The other participants looked around at each other in a quandary, but Hawkins and Betz were not moved. Someone asked if they at least could agree to "stand aside" in order to achieve a consensus decision. Hawkins and Betz felt group pressure for a resolution, and when they agreed to this everyone was relieved. Mahdi, though, "kept shaking his head" in doubt as to whether a true understanding had been reached. According to Rensenbrink the participants in the "key players" meeting then decided that as a sign of their consensus they all would sit together the next morning to present the proposal to the full GPOC group. It was near three in the morning when the meeting finally ended.

But when Rensenbrink and the others began showing up that morning they found Hawkins and Betz already there, passing out copies of their own proposal, once again a version of the "unified structure" that Hawkins and the LGN had been pushing all along. In Rensenbrink's account the others were ambushed, but in Hawkins' version he and Betz had made it clear the previous evening that they intended to do this. The supposed "consensus" proposal, as it was presented after the stage was already set by Hawkins and Betz, was seen by the assembled as a competing proposal from the faction favoring GPOC independence, not a consensus proposal at all. Hawkins and Betz sat apart from the rest contrary to what the others thought they had agreed to, reinforcing the perception that the breach had not been healed. The debate of the previous two days revived with increased intensity, until the time came when they needed to vote. The "consensus" proposal got 54% to the unified proposal's 46%, a surprising result given the number of attendees present from the LGN and other wings of the Greens, but not enough for either to pass under GPOC's two-thirds approval rule. There was to be no GPOC endorsement of a restructuring proposal as the GCoC gathering started.

The gathering itself came as an anticlimax, as some form of a unified structure now seemed inevitable. Fortunately the sense of division was allayed by a "thunderously received" general assembly speech by Ron Daniels on why he was running for President. He made clear how such a bid could help organize the grassroots, educate the public, and advance issues, effectively countering the arguments of those who had been hell-bent against the idea of national electoral engagement. Daniels also called for a national "Progressive Convention" in 1992 as a way of unifying progressives. When the gathering turned to business, the sentiment of the four hundred or so members present was against having two separate Green organizations and no such proposal was introduced. Some GPOC people blamed LGN members for the failure of GPOC to get behind a bicameral proposal, in effect losing the proposal's *raison d'être*, but Hawkins dismissed this as "nasty and divisive red-baiting."

The negotiations during the GPOC meeting did help pave the way for an accommodation of some GPOC concerns within the framework of an integrated structure, and over the next few days a small committee continued discussions toward that end. The gathering finally approved a new (and complicated) structure along with a name change to The Greens usa. The highest decision-making body was to be an annual Green Congress, composed of representatives from the dues paying locals. The Green Congress would elect delegates to a Green Council, which also was to include delegates from various identity caucuses and from the regional organizations. The latter were reduced for manageability from what had grown to some three dozen regions down to eleven. The Green Council would meet a few times a year to carry out policies and would elect a new Coordinating Committee of seven members to conduct business between Council meetings and serve as national spokespersons. GPOC became the Green Party Organizing Caucus within The Greens usa (changing the meaning of the "C" in GPOC from Committee to Caucus), and a Political Action Committee named The Green Party USA was set up as a vehicle to raise funds for and coordinate electoral activism. The PAC's board would in part be elected by the Green Congress and in part drawn from "kindred" organizations, such as for people of color, with the selection process to be worked out by yet another Structural Working Group. The working group was also charged with formulating procedures for accrediting and representing state Green parties. Lorenz and Hawkins were elected to the new Coordinating Committee, which on the whole leaned toward the left Greens, but Rensenbrink was not.

In one respect all sides got what they wanted, which was to maintain a working relationship between the state party activists and those Greens not engaged in state party work. A Mediation Council composed of experienced people selected at the annual Congress was a significant gesture born of this cooperative impulse. Cooperation was also expressed in the adoption of a nationally coordinated set of programs for local activism, one of which aimed at community control of energy generation, particularly for indigenous peoples, and another to focus on community work in Detroit during the summer of 1992. Toward the end of the gathering a new Green Justice Caucus, made up of caucuses for people of color, gays and lesbians, youth, and women, pulled people together by honoring several Greens from different parts of the movement for their contributions to the organization over the past several years. This was perhaps an emotionally satisfying conclusion, but it could not disguise the fact that the main outcome of the gathering was that the LGN and their allies had clipped the wings of GPOC by harnessing it within a stronger national structure over which the LGN had considerable influence. The crux of the matter was not whether the two factions would work together in a more cooperative fashion, but the terms under which this would take place: as equals, or with one subordinated to the other. The latter won out.

Or so it seemed. Even with its wings clipped, this bird was not so easily caged. State party organizing and petition drives had spread by then to a number of states, including Florida, New Hampshire, Delaware, Minnesota, Colorado, Idaho, Oregon, New Mexico, Arizona and Hawai'i. Many of the activists had run into opposition from the left Greens, with the Michigan effort succumbing earlier that spring, but party organizing continued to gain strength and experience over the course of the year. For example, the push to create a party in Oregon, led by Blair Bobier, promoted it as "the Pacific Party," in part to avoid left Green hostilities and in part because it was born of anti-war opposition to the Gulf War. Only later did they add "Green" to their name to become the Pacific Green Party. The California registration drive had reached about 40% of the needed voter registrations by August, and with four months left to finish began pushing hard to get there.

In addition to the state party activity, several GPOC leaders were sprinkled throughout key positions in The Greens usa. Not John Rensenbrink, who devoted his extra time to finishing a book on his ideas about the Greens and transformative politics. However, Mindy Lorenz was on the Coordinating

Committee, Barbara Rodgers-Hendricks of Florida was on the Green Council, and Greg Gerritt was secretary of the Structural Working Group for the new Green Party USA Political Action Committee.

But the disciplining of the GPOC leaders was not finished yet. Rensenbrink was publically vilified in print as not only a right-winger but a McCarthyite. Lorenz was badly outnumbered on the CC and came under personal and political attack, both on the national body and in southern California where she continued her party building work. Rodgers-Hendricks also found herself the target of verbal abuse, a scapegoat for the perceived crimes of GPOC. According to Rensenbrink, she later described this as "one of the most bitter and hurtful experiences she had ever endured." Despite problems with participation, Gerritt managed to "cobble" together a report from the Structural Working Group identifying the varying views of its contributors, including his own view that it was illegal and immoral to subject state parties to the control of nonparty activists. Instead he proposed a national electoral organization made up of independent state parties, the same way other political parties are structured in the United States. He was censured for this proposal and the Working Group abolished for failing to achieve consensus. And Dee Berry, who was trying to build a Missouri Green Party, had her campaign for Lieutenant Governor of Kansas derailed by a false accusation of stealing money while co-chair of the Prairie Greens regional.

At a loss for how to continue electoral work under such circumstances and tired of fighting continual battles with supposed allies, Rensenbrink agonized over what to do. Finally, after "a lot of anxiety and sleepless nights," he proposed in a letter to his GPOC confidants that they go back to building a party activist organization independent of The Greens usa. The response was "instant relief and acclaim," with all of them eager to shed the hostile environment they had become mired in and start anew.

Then late in the year the news hit Northern California that the state political director of the Democratic Party was returning registration cards to newly registered Greens and asking them to return to the Democratic Party. Outrage inspired many more voters to join the Greens and registration workers to intensify their efforts. By the beginning of December they had collected about 60,000 registrations, or three quarters of the minimum needed. An unexpected large donation enabled them to hire some professional signature gatherers. In combination with the volunteer workers they collected about 40,000 registrations in December alone, going some 25,000 beyond the minimum required.

On January 21, 1992, the Secretary of State of California, the most populous state in the nation, certified the Green Party of California for the state ballot. It was the first new party to do so in twenty years.

CHAPTER EIGHT

The Split

The U.S. Presidential election campaign was barely getting off the ground as 1992 rolled around. Incumbent President George H.W. Bush, the presumptive Republican nominee, was coasting on the Gulf War victory rather than actively campaigning, despite the electoral threat of a deepening recession. Texas businessman Ross Perot had not yet announced his maverick bid for the Presidency. A half dozen candidates were running for the Democratic nomination, but none of them was in the media spotlight as a clear front runner. (Arkansas Governor Bill Clinton was soon to gain national media attention, although not in a favorable light, when he was accused of marital infidelity.)

Several of the Greens' policy positions were compatible with those of various Presidential candidates, most of them long shots for election. As mentioned earlier, Ron Daniels was actively seeking the support of various groups and alternative parties. Jerry Brown, the former governor of California who had run for President twice before, was a progressive favorite in the Democratic race with a strong reformist agenda. But probably the best known candidate with a Green-compatible platform, as well as the most unexpected entrant, was Ralph Nader.

Nader was born in a small town in Connecticut in 1934, the middle of the Great Depression. He credits his strong sense of traditional values to his Lebanese immigrant parents and early exposure to town hall meetings—values like service, hard work, listening to others, independent thinking, human equality, and civic participation. He graduated from Princeton and went on to Harvard Law School while spending time working on rights issues with Native Americans and migrant workers. After a short stint in the army he did work in law, education, journalism and government consulting. Then in 1965 he shot to sudden national prominence with his exposé of automobile safety issues, the best-selling *Unsafe at Any Speed,* which inspired the passage of the National Traffic and Motor Vehicle Safety Act. Nader won an invasion of privacy suit against General Motors after learning they hired a detective to dig up dirt on him, and he used the proceeds to fund the first of his many citizen activist and consumer protection groups. By the 1970s he was a household name and one of the most admired people in the country. In 1972 prominent figures in the New Party and People's Party tried to recruit him as a Presidential candidate, but he declined, preferring to continue his activism and lobbying on behalf of citizens' and environmental causes. He even received a call from Democratic Presidential candidate George McGovern about stepping in as his running mate when Thomas Eagleton withdrew in August of that year, but Nader continued to insist his role was as a public citizen. Then in the 1980s, with the Reagan and Bush administrations in power, the national government became deaf to his lobbying and began actively undoing the kinds of regulations he had championed. A new strategy was needed.

In late November 1991, after renewed pleas to consider a Presidential run, Nader entered the electoral arena for the first time. In New Hampshire, the site of the nation's first Presidential primary for both the Democrats and the Republicans, he gave speeches promoting a set of political reform proposals and asked voters to write his name in on the ballot "not as a candidate for elective office but as an advocate for a reform agenda." This was a way of publicizing and gaining a show of support for his proposals, which included items such as term limits, campaign financing reform, easier ballot access, funding for a national taxpayers association, workers' rights, shareholder democracy, and civic education. Volunteers mobilized to support him, and over the next couple of months he travelled the state appearing before audiences "far larger than those for the candidates on the ballot," with people staying for "two or three hours" to listen to him and discuss the proposals. On a freezing day at the beginning of February he stood on the steps of the State Capitol Building in Concord to give a speech presenting what he now called the "Concord Principles:"

> Presidential campaigns have become narrow, shallow, redundant, and frantic parades and horseraces which candidates, their monetary backers, and their handlers control unilaterally, with the citizenry expected to be the bystanders and compliant voters... [W]e, the citizens of the United States...are committed to begin the work of shaping the substance of Presidential campaigns and of engaging the candidates' attention to our citizen agenda during this 1992 election year... Developing these democratic tools to strengthen citizens in their distinct roles as voters, taxpayers, consumers, workers, shareholders, and students should be very high on the list of any candidate's commitments to you.

On the day of the primary, February 18th, he received about 1.8% of the votes in each of the two dominant parties' primaries (3,054 votes from Democrats and 3,257 from Republicans), showing bipartisan support for his program. He went on to make a small showing on the Massachusetts ballot as well. Despite the trivial effect of his campaign on the election outcomes, within a few more years Nader's populist message and new willingness to engage in an electoral campaign was to have a profound effect on the prospects for a national Green party.

Not too far away in Maine that spring, John Rensenbrink finished writing his book on Green politics. In a prescient coincidence his book quoted Nader from an earlier interview on the possibility of creating a viable third party in the U.S.:

> Sure it's do-able, but you need 1,000 grassroots organizers full-time. That is the hidden chip. The Citizens' Party got 225,000 votes, and they didn't even have two organizers. You need 1,000 organizers.

The Greens were far from having such a capacity, described by Rensenbrink at the time as "a small and insignificant group of mostly middle-class whites, with a sprinkling of other people of color, scattered in small groups around the country." At that point no one was seriously proposing a national Green Party with its own Presidential candidate. The ambition of Green party electoral activists was to join the proposed Third Force of progressive groups who could mount a combined national campaign, driven by opposition to the Democrats' continued trend towards militarism and "centrist" economics. There were already a variety of efforts toward this end, with an Alliance for Our Common Future established in 1989, a conference organized by Jeremy Rifkin of the Greenhouse Crisis Foundation in early 1991, a First National People of Color Environmental Leadership meeting later that year, and the National Organization of Women holding hearings on "Responsive Democracy" around the country.

But so far the Greens were a marginal force in all this. Rensenbrink and others saw an opportunity, if only the Greens could resolve their internal issues and build an electoral arm, to be a contributor. In his book, *The Greens and the Politics of Transformation,* he argued the case for a transformation to a new, ecological way of perceiving our social situation and engaging in politics. This standpoint had been evolving within the electoral activist and spiritually-oriented ecofeminist wings of the Greens as their differences with the Left Greens sharpened over the years. Rensenbrink described the challenges and successes of the U.S. Greens in trying to realize this vision, especially the wrestling over the party versus movement dilemma. In two appendixes he took account of the 1991 Elkins Gathering and the success of the California Green Party in obtaining ballot access, and he was still offering the possibility of a cooperating relationship between different wings of the Greens: "Alignment of strategies is the creative way forward, not the integration of strategies." Yet by the time the book was published events had overtaken this optimistic assessment.

At its meeting in Boston in February of the previous year, GPOC had planned a March 1992 conference for training in electoral activism. Now that many GPOC leaders had been driven from The Greens usa, they met with a somewhat altered agenda. Held at the Hartland Center in Kansas City over the course of six days, during the first half of the conference they took the plunge and created a new independent organization, the Green Politics Network (GPN). The new organization adopted the Four Pillars of European Green Parties (Ecology, Social Justice, Nonviolence and Participatory Democracy) and resolved on four goals:

1. to facilitate the creation of an "Confederation of Independent State Green Parties,"
2. to contribute to the development of a Third Force coalition of allied groups and organizations,
3. to be a protective zone against abusive behaviors ("how we treat each other is as important as achieving our goals"),
4. and to offer a space for people to connect with "the spiritual universe."

Among the GPN founders were Rensenbrink and Greg Gerritt from Maine, Mindy Lorenz from California, Dee Berry and Ben Kjelshus from Missouri, Sue Conti from Virginia, Barbara Rodgers-Hendricks from Florida, Suleiman Madhi from Georgia, Blair Bobier from Oregon, Betty Zisk from Massachusetts, and Annie Goeke and Tom Linzey from Pennsylvania. During the second half of the conference invitees from more than a dozen other parties and organizations joined them for talks about the Third Force project. Together they committed to building an alternative political force and to continue conversations toward this end. This was to be the first in a series of Third Force conventions held over the next few years.

After the conference thirteen of the GPN members published a "Rationale for Launching a Green Politics Network" in the *Greens Bulletin*. They charged that the national Green organization had become "as oppressive as the patriarchal society we are committed to transforming" and entangled in "the old power and control games." They were taking a different path in order to take advantage of the opportunity to be "a national catalyst with a holistic, post-capitalist and post-socialist politics." Expressing their intention to work as a "parallel organization" with the Greens usa, they hoped to be able to make it a "cooperating relationship."

Despite this ostensible olive branch, clearly the four goals of GPN were not only a proclamation of independence for the electoral wing of the Green movement but a rebuke to behaviors they attributed to the LGN. The GPN founders regarded the new organization as more of an incubator of various projects than a competitor to the Greens usa, but predictably the Left Greens did not see it this way. The LGN vilified GNP organizers as "renegades," "rightists," "elitists," and "politicians" and tried to deter other organizations from working with them. They charged that the GPN was out to replace the Greens usa and presenting itself as a national Green Party when there weren't yet more than a handful of legally recognized state Green parties. (The Green Party of Hawai'i gained ballot access in May, exceeding the 4,533 signature requirement by submitting 8,000, and in June the Arizona Green Party also won state recognition via petition signatures.)

Howie Hawkins produced his own analysis of the struggles within the movement over the preceding eight years, published at the beginning of the year. His article, "North American Greens Come of Age: Statism vs. Munici-palism," painted the organizational fights as really over different strategies for confronting a centralized corporate state. He outlined the historical dilemma of opposition activists facing two unpalatable choices. One was to oppose the state from the outside at the risk of marginalization and relative impotence. The other was to seek seats within the government at the risk of becoming co-opted as partners in the management of the corporate state. He saw the GPOC leaders as blindly followed the latter path, while the LGN was offering an entirely new strategy of winning local offices and building local democratic assemblies as the foundation of an opposition force. The confederal municipalist position had decisively won this battle:

> The significance of the Elkins conference is that it broke through the stalemate between these two views at the national level... As the Elkins conference ran its course, the GPOC leadership saw that they were a small minority. Rather than risk a vote on competing proposals, they agreed to a compromise proposal that embodied the essential grassroots, participatory, and confederal structures which the left had wanted.

Regardless of Hawkins' claim of organizational victory, the problem he and his allies still faced was how to incorporate the rising tide of electoral activism into the Greens usa. Gerritt's Structural Working Group had been replaced by a New Ad Hoc Working Group of three people appointed by the Coordinating Committee. Taking up the advice of a consultant on nonprofits to the Budget and Finance Committee, the Working Group recommended that the Greens usa be incorporated as a political party and renamed The Greens/Green Party USA (G/GPUSA), with the Green Council becoming the Green National Committee. Their recommendations were adopted by the Green Congress at the gathering held at Augsburg College in Minneapolis,

Minnesota that July. This move served as an obvious counter to any claim of GPN to be the national Green Party.

One of the central issues for the 1992 Congress was if and how voters registered in the new state parties would be represented in the national organization, which had been set up so as to be controlled by dues paying members from its local chapters. The Green Party of California, for example, had over 35,000 voters registered with the party but only a few dozen were dues paying members of what was now G/GPUSA. The Congress decided to allow state level Green organizations, whether state parties or confederations of locals, to designate themselves "regions" entitled to two representatives each on the Green National Committee. This would facilitate a shift from regions to states as organizing units and better accommodate state Green parties as they were created. They also set up an Electoral Working Group to replace the Green Party USA PAC and tasked it with accrediting a state party if it met three requirements: (1) it agreed to hold itself, its candidates, and Green elected officials to the Ten Key Values, (2) it agreed to enter a conflict resolution process on the request of any Green local or state confederation active in that state, and (3) it was not opposed by majority of G/GPUSA-affiliated locals in the state. These conditions exhibited the LGN's abiding goal of subjecting party activists to "grassroots" movement activists within a unified organizational structure. Thus far no state party had affiliated with the organization.

A three-day Green Economics Training program was held just before the gathering, funded by a grant that limited the event to educational purposes. A little over 200 people attended workshops on topics such as "Basic Economics for Activists," "Transitional Economics," and "Building a Green Society through Economic Restructuring," with presenters from a variety of organizations including the Center for Popular Economics, the International Alliance for Sustainable Agriculture, a Minnesota co-op and an intentional community. This was in line with the left Greens' longtime emphasis on economic questions and helped the Congress in a rewriting of the Economics plank of their platform. Other significant events at the Minneapolis Congress included a kickoff march and demonstration against the Northern States Power Company's alleged environmental racism, a contentious change of the Key Value "postpatriarchal values" to "feminism," and an expansion of the Detroit Summer Project to Syracuse and Los Angeles.

That fall the argument over electoral versus movement activism popped up again in the left Green journal *Regeneration*, showing that despite the banishment of the GPN leaders the debate was far from settled within G/GPUSA. Proponents of an electoral focus argued that movement building had reached a peak in many areas and seemed to be withering for lack of a clear direction, as most Green concerns were already being covered by various single issue organizations. The holistic, multi-issue approach the Greens favored would best be accomplished in the electoral arena, where no other contemporary alternative party had had the multi-year, widespread electoral successes of the Greens. Opponents countered that this approach rested on "the myth that the system works" while it distracts people from working for fundamental change by opposing the established order. The two dominant parties had a history of co-opting any popular positions from an alternative party and then abandoning those positions after the pressure of serious competition was destroyed. Howie Hawkins and Suleiman Mahdi contended that a party had to be rooted in a movement and accountable to it, otherwise it would sell out for success or crumble due to electoral failures. True power, they argued—power in corporations, banks, universities and the mass media—is impervious to change by mere elections.

Meanwhile the election year wore on, with signs of voter rebellion against the status quo everywhere. Conservative populist Pat Buchanan ran a surprisingly strong primary campaign against President Bush, and Jerry Brown survived to become the main threat to front runner Bill Clinton on the Democratic side. Ron Daniels got on the ballot for the Peace and Freedom Party in California, the Labor and Farm Party in Wisconsin, the Independent Party in New Jersey, his own Campaign for a New Tomorrow Party in Iowa and Utah, and organized write-in votes in several other states. His campaign also generated a National Independent Politics Summit at the People's Progressive Convention in Michigan that August. In attendance were representatives of the National Committee for Independent Political Action, G/GPUSA, the California Peace and Freedom Party, and dozens of other organizations. However, Daniels received a negligible less than one-tenth a percent of the vote in the general election. Ralph Nader assessed the results of his own brief campaign in *The Nation* that July, taking note of future possibilities:

> In a small way, our experience in New Hampshire and later in Massachusetts confirms that a larger effort in future contests could switch the pre-election dynamic from candidate-side to citizen-side campaigns. It could end the feeble, marble-mouthed, two-party politics that have turned off so many Americans and result in a strengthened democracy.

But the most glaring evidence of voter revolt was the widespread enthusiasm for Ross Perot's idiosyncratic campaign. Despite an abrupt departure and late reentry into the race, he won 18.9% of the popular vote in November, the strongest showing of an alternative candidate since Theodore Roosevelt's Progressive Party bid in 1912. That caught people's attention and spurred the perennial hope of breaking the two-party hold on elections.

Less noticed but still notable was the growth in the number of Greens running for and winning elections. Ninety-three candidates—many but not most of them GPN members—ran in thirteen states, far surpassing the 1990 numbers. Twenty Green candidates won, including eleven of forty-four who ran in California. In addition to campaigns for local offices, there were several for higher offices. Running for seats in the U.S. Congress were Mindy Lorenz and Blasé Bonpane in California, Barbara Rodgers-Hendricks in Florida, Blair Bobier in Oregon, Jonathan Carter in Maine, Jeff Barrow in Missouri, and Carolyn Campbell in Arizona. Dee Berry ran a petition drive in Missouri to get on the ballot for Lieutenant Governor. Linda Martin ran for U.S. Senate on the new ballot line of Green Party of Hawai'i and won 13.7% of the vote, the all-time high for a Green candidate running for a national office until 1997. Also in Hawai'i a co-founder of the state party, Keiko Bonk, became the first Green Party candidate to win a partisan election when she won a county council seat on the Big Island. Furthermore, in New Mexico, where Abraham Guttman won over 40% of the vote in his race for a state legislative seat, the Greens managed to collect the 4,000 signatures required to become a state-registered political party.

For a growing number of Greens, state party building and election campaigns were where the action was. Mike Feinstein of Santa Monica was excited by the Green electoral successes, particularly in California, and took on a leading role in building upon the momentum. Born in 1958, Feinstein was adopted from a Greek orphanage and raised in a suburb of Minneapolis by his new American parents. After college he moved to Southern California, where he joined the Westside Greens of the Santa Monica/West Los Angeles area in 1988. He became co-host of the local Pacifica radio show "Green Perspectives" in 1989 and the following year was one of the co-founders of the Green Party of California. Following the 1992 elections he invited candidates, campaign managers and electoral-minded Greens to a February conference to be held in his city.

The "Green Parties of the West" conference attracted about one hundred people, mostly from the states which now had ballot access: Alaska, California, Hawai'i, Arizona and New Mexico. The conference focused primarily on lessons learned in the campaigns and plans for serious races and continued party-building in the future. Among the presenters were Keiko Bonk from Hawai'i and Kelly Weaverling, who had won the mayoral seat in Cordova, Alaska, in 1991. Topics of discussion included running to win in local races, running for higher offices to reach new people, coalition building with potential allies, competing against Democrats, and joining a Third Force Presidential campaign in 1996. The conference attendees found themselves blessedly free of disputes about internal processes and opposition to electoral activism, with Feinstein describing the latter absence as "an incredible breath of fresh air for those who want to seriously pursue Green electoral strategies."

Close upon the heels of this event was the second GPN/Third Force conference, held across the country at Bowdoin College in Brunswick, Maine. Titled "Doing It the Grass Roots Way," it was organized by faculty member Rensenbrink and Becky Koulouros, the office coordinator of the Environmental Studies Program. Again many Green candidates and activists were present, including Senate candidate Linda Martin from Hawai'i, Mayor Kelly Weaverling, Mike Feinstein reporting on the Santa Monica conference, and candidates from Florida, Maine, Missouri, and Rhode Island. Also participating were representatives of Ron Daniels' Campaign for a New Tomorrow, Ross Perot's campaign, the Center for Voting and Democracy,[7] and Sam Smith of the *Progressive Review*, who noted "a stunning absence of radical posturing" at the conference. A focal point of the discussions was asking what an alternative politics should look like. It had to be about more than just winning office, but "a way to change the dynamics and the structure of political parties and campaigning in the United States."

The GPN members still weren't certain how they would do this, but they were more certain than ever that a door to it had opened.

---

[7] The organization changed its name from Citizens for Proportional Representation, and was later to become FairVote.

CHAPTER NINE

Aiming Higher

Two key projects were on the agenda of GPN. One was to assist in the Third Force effort to consolidate forces behind an independent Presidential candidate. The other was to spur the development of state Green parties and bring them into a confederation. Among the speakers at the February Bowdoin College conference was Tony Affigne, who gave a "rousing" speech on grassroots campaign organizing, a subject he knew well. As an independent candidate for the Providence City Council in 1982 and the Citizen's Party candidate for Governor in 1986, he made local history as Rhode Island's first Latino candidate for public office. Affigne had become a Green party activist a couple of years earlier and recently joined Greg Gerritt of Maine in leading the GPN effort to bring the state parties together.

Gerritt had already produced a blueprint for this in his report from the Structural Working Group of the Greens usa, for which he had been censured by Charlie Betz. Gerritt and Affigne salvaged the idea and developed it into a proposal, "Articles of Confederation of the Green Parties of the United States," which they began circulating to the state parties. The rules for affiliation were less demanding than those of G/GPUSA, entailing acceptance of the Ten Key Values, democratic governance, and a vote to affiliate taken at a state convention. The Missouri Green Party signed on in January of 1993.

The Maine Green Party followed in March, and the Green Party of Rhode Island, which Affigne had co-founded the previous year, joined in April. In June he brought the idea out west for the plenary of the Green Party of California, where it was discussed informally but not put on the agenda. That summer a headline in the first issue of the GPN journal *Green Horizon* announced "A Confederation of State Green Parties Takes Shape," but this was a bit premature. Gerritt contacted several other state parties that fall but found a reluctance to affiliate with either GPN's Confederation or G/GPUSA until the perceived competition between them had been sorted out.

While progress on the confederation idea had stalled, GPN continued moving forward with its other activities. These included a retreat titled "Ecotreat '93" in Kansas City that April and a second retreat in June 1994 in Chocawhatchee Bay, Florida. These were primarily to provide a relaxed setting for community building among its members and allies. A bigger event was the third GPN/Third Force convention which took place in Oakland, California that same month. The Oakland convention, "New Politics '94: Nuts and Bolts for State and Local Victory," was organized by Hugh Chapot, Affigne, Rensenbrink, Linda Martin and Sam Smith. It brought together more than fifty people from state Green Parties, the New Party, Labor Party Advocates, the Patriot Party, the Peace and Freedom Party, the Center for Responsive Politics, Common Cause, the Center for Voting and Democracy, and other groups. A prominent theme was the electoral barriers to alternative parties and strategies to overcome them, such a proportional representation and fusion voting. By 1994 GPN had grown to only forty members, but it had built extensive contacts with state Green party and other alternative party activists around the country.

Nineteen ninety-four was of course an election year, and each of the five state Green parties which had already achieved ballot status had to meet specific requirements to retain it. The Alaskan party exceeded their state's requisite vote threshold with Jim Sykes' 3.9% for governor, as the California party did with Margaret Garcia's 3.8% for Secretary of State. New Mexico had a threshold of 5% for a statewide office, and the party exceeded it in three separate races: Roberto Mondragon with 10.4% for Governor, Lorenzo Garcia with 32.7% for State Treasurer, and Patricia Wolff with 11.7% for Public Lands Commissioner. However, in neighboring Arizona the party failed to meet the required number of voters registered with the party and lost its status. The Hawai'i party was not able to retain its ballot status either.

There were compensating victories. Rensenbrink worked on Johnathan Carter's bid to become Governor of Maine, which garnered 6.4% of the vote and finally added Maine to the list of states in which Green parties qualified for the ballot. And in Colorado Phil Hufford received 1.5% of the votes for Governor, not nearly enough to reach the 10% threshold to achieve ballot status, but the state party met the various requirements to become a "Qualified Political Organization," which allowed voters to register with it. In Hawai'i Keiko Bonk won re-election to her county council seat and Toni Wurst got an impressive 41% of the vote in an unsuccessful bid for state representative. Other significant races for the Greens that year included Terri Williams' upset victory to become mayor of Webster Grove, Missouri, and Greg Gerritt's second run for the Maine state legislature. He surpassed the 16% he got in 1986 with 20.2% this time around, once again running against both a Democrat and a Republican. All in all, the state Green parties were holding ground and fielding candidates who often defied expectations.

As for the self-proclaimed national Green party, even as Green electoral activity grew, G/GPUSA numbers shrank. Dues-paying memberships were falling during this period, receding from a high of 3,000 to just around 1,000. In addition to GPN sympathizers dropping out, many of the Greens engaged in local and state electoral activism saw no need to belong to the national organization. Those who were new to the Green movement came in through election activity and generally had little familiarly with G/GPUSA. The organization came out of 1992 with a debt of over $32,000, more than half attributable to the costs of the Minneapolis gathering, with other costs due to multiple changes in the staffing and location of the Clearing House. The official journal *Green Letter* was in financial straits, and it began shifting its reporting from the Greens' activities to broader social topics in hope of gaining subscriptions. This produced a death cycle as less coverage of the organization resulted in a greater sense of disconnection and loss of interest by members. Green candidates and electoral campaigns avoided G/GPUSA because of the attempts of its dwindling membership to control them. Only the Alaska Green Party had affiliated with it, and that only provisionally, until later the Green Party of New York, founded in 1992 and led by Howie Hawkins, joined.

The August 1993 G/GPUSA gathering in Syracuse, New York attracted a good 300 people, which was encouraging. Some camped at Earthwise Education Center, run by a former Black Panther on his family's organic farm. The farm ran sustainable agriculture training programs for urban youth and the homeless and owned an inner city soul food restaurant, Vera's Place, which provided meals for the gathering with the sessions held on an adjacent empty lot. The theme was "Green Cities and Green Justice," with workshops on topics such as Green cities, organizing, running campaigns, and organic farming. But when it was time for the Green Congress to meet, discussions turned to finances and bylaws and became heated and acrimonious.

The next year's gathering, held in August 1994 in Boise, Idaho, chose the theme "Embracing Common Ground: Celebrating Human and Bio-Diversity," with workshops on sexual and ecological diversity. This one brought in a paltry twenty-five members, with voting decisions controlled by a small number of members from LGN-dominated locals holding proxies. Once again they bogged down over questions of money and organizational rules, the latter of which Steve Schmidt characterized as "intrusive, overarching, complicated and considered by many to be unworkable." He also described the G/GPUSA meetings of this time period as "infamous for strident disagreement, member blocking under consensus rules and list and voting irregularities."

The LGN declined even more precipitously. They had never numbered much more than 300 members, although they had plenty of allies in the movement, but now that they had effective control of G/GPUSA many members saw no need for a separate organization. Anarchist-oriented members departed as the left Greens became more engaged in the rule-bound G/GPUSA; their ally the Youth Greens, for example, lost members and by 1994 had dissolved. Only twenty-five members attended the LGN fourth national convention in Iowa City in May of 1992, and a mere six attended the May 1993 convention in Toronto. The *Left Green Notes* lost income and submissions and ended by 1993.

Howie Hawkins was correct in 1992 when he said that the left Greens had won the battle within the national organization, but in doing so they lost the war. From the first stirring around the idea of a Green political organization in 1984 the left Greens had attempted to capture it for their strategic vision of confederal municipalism. Once they succeeded the mass of grassroots Greens deserted it for state party organizing instead. The future of the Green movement was slipping out of their control and toward that envisioned by their supposedly defeated rivals, John Rensenbrink and the others who had persisted in the strategy of building state parties for electoral activism at all levels.

And that included the highest level. With 1996 on the horizon the eyes of electoral activists began turning to the Presidency. Incumbent Bill Clinton was sure to run for re-election, leaving little room for progressives to make a serious bid for the Democratic nomination. Progressives had few illusions about Clinton. Steve Schmidt had been closely involved in Jerry Brown's 1992 Presidential campaign and was the chief author of his reform platform, which was Green-friendly and included positions from the Rainbow Coalition. After the election he brought it to Ron Brown, the chair of the Democratic Party and soon-to-be Commerce Secretary in the Clinton administration. "It was rejected in terms too rude to repeat," Schmidt said. Convinced by Ross Perot's vote numbers that new electoral possibilities had opened, Schmidt decided it was time to change tracks. In 1994 he switched from the Democrats to the Green Party of New Mexico. This decision led to one of several crisscrossing paths in the complicated journey of the Greens to a role in the 1996 Presidential election.

Abraham Guttman, a co-founder of the New Mexico party, recruited Schmidt to run for Lieutenant Governor on a ticket with Green gubernatorial candidate Roberto Mondragon, another Guttman recruit. Mondragon was a prime catch for the Green Party: a prominent Democrat who had twice served as Lieutenant Governor of the state. Schmidt also lent his talents to process of creating a state party platform, which drew media attention and became a key part of their '94 campaign. Together Schmidt and Mondragon polled 10.4% of the vote, which led to credit/blame for the loss of pro-business Democratic incumbent Bruce King to Republican newcomer Gary Johnson. The campaign also activated a lot of Greens and raised the party's profile both statewide and nationally. As mentioned earlier, two other statewide Green candidates won even higher shares of the vote for their offices. The election results required the state government to declare the Green Party of New Mexico a "major" party under its election laws, a stunning achievement for a new party. Another achievement was the success of Cris Moore, a young physicist in Santa Fe, as a local-level candidate. The city had an exceptionally active Green local, which had run campaigns for property tax relief for low-income residents, a work-hours currency exchange, a living wage, and tenant rights. Moore rode popular support for this activism straight onto a nonpartisan seat on the city council. Guttman, Schmidt, and Moore worked closely together in building the state party during the election year. The trio now began talking strategy on a larger scale.

In January 1995, with the next year's Presidential race in mind, Schmidt contacted two California Greens who shared the New Mexicans' interest in developing a national strategy. One of them was Mike Feinstein, who had convened the Santa Monica conference of early 1993, and other was Greg Jan, an activist in Oakland. They discussed how the New Mexico experience could inform a national strategy to build the party by drafting a national Green platform and finding a "name" candidate to run for President on it. They then got to work. Schmidt managed to obtain private funding to support his platform writing while Feinstein and Jan developed a proposal for building a "Forty State Green Party." The idea was that by running a Presidential candidate with a credible platform in multiple states, Green parties could attract interest, recruit and activate new members, and gain ballot access where they did not already have it.

Meanwhile Cris Moore, with the Santa Fe experience as a model for how direct action and electoral campaigns could work together, used this as an opportunity to bring the various wings of the Greens back together. He persuaded the New Mexico party to call for a "National Green Conference" to be held in Albuquerque in late July. Moore had become somewhat disenchanted with the left Greens of G/GPUSA, so instead of making this another Green Gathering for that troubled organization, he also invited participants from GPN, state Green parties, Campus Greens, and other groups. The widespread popularity of the proposal induced G/GPUSA and others go along with it. With its poorly attended 1994 Green Congress fresh in mind, G/GPUSA piggybacked on the Green Conference idea by scheduling its national Congress to be held immediately afterward.

GPN was also busy planning for the Presidential election, with the next GPN/Third Force conference set to take place June 1st-4th. Rensenbrink had been in regular phone contact with Feinstein since the 1993 Bowdoin conference, hashing over various Green party affairs. He kept pushing the idea of a Confederation of State Green Parties while Feinstein resisted, still wanting G/GPUSA to be involved if the California party was to lend its weight to a plan for the state parties to join together. Shortly before the June conference they talked about how the 1993 founding of the European Federation of Green Parties had been preceded by a loose network called "The Green Coordination." This network was for discussions only, with each European Green party having equal representation. Rensenbrink and Feinstein talked about the possibility of something similar involving GPN, G/GPUSA, and state parties. The idea was to create a space to sort out differences in order for the movement as a whole to move forward. The planned Albuquerque conference engendered hope that this plan might actually lead somewhere, and over the intervening weeks several state parties agreed to it.

The June 1995 GPN/Third Force conference, "Third Parties '96," was held in Washington, D.C., their fourth foray in this direction. Again there were people from a variety of parties and organizations, including the New Party, the Libertarian Party, Ross Perot's "United We Stand" organization, the Labor Party, and the Socialist Party. Altogether there were over a hundred participants from some forty-three organizations, including twenty-six alternative parties. Together they produced a "Common Ground Declaration" with agreement on seventeen policy positions and at least 60% agreement on several others. The easy ones were items like proportional representation, campaign finance reform, easier ballot access, and ending corporate subsidies. Progressive items like sustainable energy production, women's rights, and community-based decision making met more resistance. The conference received extensive media coverage from outlets such as C-SPAN, Pacifica Radio, NPR, *The Nation*, and *The Progressive*, demonstrating the continued interest in a viable electoral alternative to the two-party duopoly.

Conversations continued at an after-event for relaxation at Sam Smith's Washington home, where Rensenbrink and Feinstein raised their Green Coordination idea. It met with wide approval, including that of Cris Moore, initiator of the Albuquerque conference. Tom Cadorette, who belonged to both GPN and G/GPUSA, volunteered to get it on the agenda of the G/GPUSA Green Congress to be held following that conference. So far things were looking hopeful for the various initiatives to bring Greens together for the upcoming election year.

Later in June Feinstein, Jan, and Schmidt sent an email to Greens around the country outlining their idea for building a Forty State Green Party, which despite similarities was a different direction than that underlying the Third Force concept. Both looked to a platform and a Presidential candidate to unify an alternative political force, but the former aimed at unifying the Greens while the latter aimed at unifying alternative parties. Feinstein et al argued that the public favored the concept of a "third" party and that of the variety of left-leaning parties out there only the Greens had a decade-long experience of running candidates and winning offices.[8] They referenced the New Mexico success in building their party by running a name candidate at the top of the ticket and included a survey of views on potential Presidential candidates. They also asked if state parties or Green locals would assist with such a campaign. The responses indicated strong support for the proposal among the minority who answered, but no clear favorite among the suggested candidates. Rensenbrink and Feinstein's idea for a Green Coordination was also circulated via the internet in advance of the Albuquerque conference.

The National Green Conference convened in New Mexico at the end of July with over 230 people from thirty-two states, plus representatives from Green Parties in Canada, Australia, Mexico and Niger. There were workshops and speeches on a variety of topics, both direct action and election-related, including a report from Linda Martin on the GPN/Third Force meeting the previous month. The Forty State Green Party proposal met with a mixed reception. Feinstein presented data showing that, including the few state parties which already had it, gaining ballot access over the next year was feasible in twenty-three states plus the District of Columbia. G/GPUSA members repeated familiar arguments against running a presidential candidate, principally that it was a top-down vs. a grassroots approach to building a party. But the discussion was highjacked by a left Green who proposed a resolution to nominate death row inmate and left-wing *cause celébrè* Mumia Abu-Jamal

---

[8] The right-leaning Libertarian Party had a longer history and more success in electing candidates than the Greens.

as President. The resolution almost gained a majority vote. Although it needed two-thirds to pass, it succeeded in putting the electoral-minded Greens on notice that many Greens still had very different views on election campaigns than they did. Discussion of Feinstein and Rensenbrink's proposal for a Green Coordination was undermined by the same group supporting the Abu-Jamal nomination. They were skeptical of a dialogue with GPN about Green unity, given that GPN had split from the national organization just after the latter had created a new organizational structure specifically aimed at unifying the Greens.

The conference succeeded in bringing Greens together for conversations and made the national news, but it failed to win agreement on any specific plan other than meeting again the next year. The GPN contingent did vote to endorse the Forty State concept, notwithstanding their commitment to the Third Force approach. And the G/GPUSA Green Congress following the conference approved a revised version of the Green Coordination idea, renaming it a "Green Roundtable" and stressing that it would have no decision-making power. Otherwise there were few grounds for continued optimism. GPN leaders were not terribly shocked when G/GPUSA failed to follow up on the Green Roundtable idea after the conference. Although there were many balls in motion for the 1996 election, they were in the hands of diverse players not sure yet which game they were playing.

Linda Martin, one of the principals in GPN's Third Force efforts, left the Albuquerque conference facing an unwelcome task. Martin had begun her activism in the 1980s while living in Southern California, starting with land-use issues, affordable housing and Planned Parenthood. After moving to Hawai'i with her husband at the start of the new decade, she joined the Green Party of Hawai'i and became co-chair, helping lead their petition drive until they succeeded in getting on the ballot in 1992. She ran for U.S. Senate that year, winning nearly 14% of the vote and securing their ballot line for another election cycle. By the time she moved to Virginia with her husband the following year, Martin had become committed to building a national Green Party and actually winning elections. She temporarily returned to Hawai'i to co-chair Toni Wurst's campaign for the state house, helping her get to 41% of the vote. "I guess when people hear Green Party, they expect someone really radical or something," she once told a reporter. "We are the mainstream of the future." Her aim of "mainstreaming" the Greens fit in well with GPN, and she was the principal organizer of the Third Parties '96 conference in Washington the previous month.

At the end of the Third Parties '96 conference she was pleased by its creation of a platform—or "proto-platform" as Tony Affigne labelled it—but uncertain about how to use it to move forward. As the attendees gathered up their belongings to leave the ballroom a stranger approached her with his hand extended. He was Robert Hager, a public interest lawyer, and he told her "We have to get together." She didn't remember seeing him during the event and didn't know what to make of this at first. "I'm a friend of Sam Smith's," he added. "He suggested we meet." Smith was part of the Third Force team so Martin took Hager's number and called him the next week.

When they met at a local pizza place he explained his idea for a "New Mainstream" agenda, intended to bring together voters from both the left and the right who felt unrepresented by the two dominant parties. So far this tracked with the Third Force approach and the Green slogan, "not left, not right, but in front." Hager insisted that the right leader, or set of leaders, was necessary to bring the coalition together, as platforms don't mean much to the average voter. Martin was impressed by his analysis, as well as his Harvard law degree, green lifestyle, and background in anti-nuclear activism and international legal consulting. He promised to put his plan in writing before the Albuquerque conference and get it to Martin so she could present it. She agreed to advocate for it among the GPN members at the meeting.

Several phone conversations later Hager delivered the goods: an eight-page fax titled "A Popular-Conservative Party to Contest the 1996 Election." She found it to be written with the precision of a legal brief, the argument summed up thus: "With the end of the cold war it is time to drop the sterile left-right paradigm and return to the basic democratic struggle of majority versus elite control of government." This was closer to Perot-style populism than to a left front against the rightward turn of national politics. She took copies to the Albuquerque conference and distributed them to her GPN allies, where it met an "icy" reception. Hager was an unknown outsider, and his openness to the anti-government right was off-putting to a group that was basically on the left end of the political spectrum, despite their slogan.

Breaking the news to Hager was the unwelcome task that Martin faced on her way home after the meeting. When they got together again he took the news in stride, saying that he would lobby Green leaders himself to bring them on board. He added, to Martin's surprise, that he would have to work fast because he had to leave in late November for work in Kyrgyzstan. Then he revealed one more piece of his plan: he had someone in mind as the only person who could bring his idea to fruition as a Presidential candidate, and he had good reasons to think that person could be persuaded to accept the role.

That person was Ralph Nader.

CHAPTER TEN

Nader '96 and the Second Founding

Hager explained to Martin that he knew Ralph Nader, and that Nader wanted to move President Clinton to the left on certain policy issues. Nader had run some ballot initiatives in California and was popular in the state. Hager saw this as an opening to persuade Nader to run for President on the Green Party of California ballot line, as a confrontation with Clinton there could give Nader the leverage to move the President in his direction. Martin, familiar with Nader's lessened influence in the Capitol and reputation as a miserly taskmaster to employees of his public interest groups, was not so sure he was the right person for the Greens, but she kept her reservations to herself. Hager promised to pursue Nader until he signed the California filing papers by their final due date—November 27, which was also the last day Hager could still catch a flight to do his job in Kyrgyzstan.

Martin left this to Hager and turned to another task she had. The National Independent Politics Network (NIPN), which had grown out of Ron Daniel's 1992 Presidential run, had been dormant in 1993-94 due to lack of funds, but its steering committee came back to life in 1995. The NIPN and GPN both wanted to pull together a coalition to support an independent run for the Presidency, but this time around their efforts were somewhat in tension with each other. As of August their differences were still submerged and NIPN was making efforts to coordinate with GPN, including moving the date of their own planned conference so as not to conflict with the Third Parties '96 conference. Representatives of NIPN attended the latter conference and invited Martin to their own August Summit in Pittsburg, which Martin accepted. They also created a coordinating committee to work with GPN in contacting potential Presidential candidates. Both groups reached out to several of their targets, including Jesse Jackson, Jerry Brown, Noam Chomsky, Nader, and Jim Hightower, a nationally syndicated columnist and progressive activist. Hightower declined, and others didn't respond.

Meanwhile Hager lobbied Green leaders via phone and internet about his plan to draft Nader as a Presidential candidate. Mike Feinstein, seeing a correspondence between Hager's plan and the 40-State Green Party concept, jumped at the prospect. Absent exciting electoral campaigns, party activism tended to wane; the California party was barely able to meet its fifty-person quorum at state meetings that year. Feinstein and his allies worked within the party and at a September plenary got it to set up a "receptive" process to respond quickly if any potential Presidential candidates declared their intention to seek the party's ballot line. For his part, Hager actually stationed himself in the anteroom to Nader's Washington office, hoping to buttonhole Nader personally before Hager had to leave the States.

This must have borne fruit, as in October an article appeared in the *Chicago Tribune* quoting Nader as saying he would consider being on the California ballot due to Clinton's vacillation on particular legislative issues. By early November the California Greens had sent a letter inviting him to be on their ballot line, with the additional signatures of forty-five state leaders of environmental, consumer, and other progressive organizations. When Nader responded affirmatively to the invitation, the receptive process of voting by state party county representatives started in motion. Suddenly the pieces were starting to fall in place. The Californians submitted the papers putting Nader on their primary ballot, and Nader issued a statement on November

27th—the same day Hager departed for Kyrgyzstan. The statement read:

> I intend to stand with others around the country as a catalyst for the creation of a new model of electoral politics, not to run in any campaign. Californians deserve a campaign that will practice taking the corrosive impact of special interest money out of politics at the same time that it preaches campaign finance reform. This effort will focus on removing such money from elections, and ending the corporate welfare and other privileges that it buys. I will not seek nor accept any campaign contributions.

In talks with the Greens Nader was adamant that this should be a citizen-led campaign, not a candidate-led campaign. He wanted to keep his spending on campaign activities under the Federal Election Commission's $5,000 threshold, which if exceeded subjected him to a host of regulations and reporting requirements. He was to be an unofficial candidate while it would be up to party members and other volunteers to do the bulk of the campaign work without his direct participation. It was an odd way to run for office, but it proved to be beneficial to the Greens by forcing them to work their organizing muscles.

The Third Parties '96 team was meeting in Boulder, Colorado at that same time to follow up on their June conference and prepare for another conference scheduled for Washington, D.C., in early January. On the last day of their meeting they learned of Nader's decision. Rensenbrink and the other attendees were excited about the Nader announcement and left Boulder enthused about the prospects for their January conference. In December Rensenbrink had the Maine party issue its own invitation to Nader to be on their ballot. Rensenbrink and Martin also wrote to invite him to the Third Parties '96 conference, and two days before it started Rensenbrink was able to reach Nader by phone. They met for lunch the next day, where Nader agreed to be on the ballot in Maine, as he put it, to help the party grow, advance the prospects of alternative parties, and "send a message" to President Clinton. He would not yet commit to being on the ballot in additional states, but he did say he would address their conference on the following day.

"Third Parties '96, Round Two" convened on Friday, January 5th, 1996, again with Linda Martin as the chief organizer. As it turned out, Nader had come down with a cold overnight and could not attend. During the first two days they held workshops on elections-related matters and continued work on their Common Ground Declaration, the "proto-platform" created at their previous conference. Sunday was scheduled for discussions of Nader's candidacy and strengthening the Third Force coalition. But three feet of snow fell that night, grounding buses, trains and other traffic and preventing an in-person meeting. Greens scattered among hotels and host homes around the area started phoning the conference leaders, urging them to find a way to go forward with a national Presidential campaign despite the impossibility of a formal session that day. Nine of the leaders, including Rensenbrink, Martin, Affigne, Feinstein, Greg Jan of Oakland and Dee Berry, teleconferenced about their predicament. They had the sense from discussions over the last two days that there was wide agreement about supporting a Presidential campaign that year, and even about Nader as the head of the ticket. They tentatively agreed to set up a Washington, D.C., Clearinghouse for networking and legal advice to state parties seeking to put Nader on the ballot. They also agreed to set up another conference for later that year. Although they intended to solicit buy-in from the other conference participants over the weeks to come, this was a unilateral decision that in effect cemented the Greens' first entry into a nationwide U.S. Presidential campaign.

Although the GPN leaders were swept with elation by these developments, with Martin even volunteering to head the Clearinghouse for the draft Nader movement, not everyone was happy about it. The tensions with NIPN came out in a January 31st letter they sent to the Third Parties '96 team, as well as in the responses from Rensenbrink and Hugh Chapot later in

February. NIPN complained of the duplication of coalition-building efforts and neglect in coordination, while questioning a strategy that made alliances with conservative parties and the widely distrusted Patriot Party.[9] Rensenbrink in turn emphasized "diversity" and "autonomy" in collaboration, still hoping to set old ideological categories aside for what GPN regarded as a new way of approaching politics. NIPN members were also skeptical of Nader and what they perceived as his lack of interest on issues of importance to people of color. Later Rensenbrink complained of the NIPN people being "particular" about who was or was not a progressive, shunning the label much as he and his allies had shied from the "socialist" label. In many respects their differences mirrored those GPN had with the left Greens, and in fact, in addition to Ron Daniels and the other signers of the NIPN letter, Howie Hawkins' name was affixed to it. By spring NIPN and the Third Parties team had parted ways. Other groups also peeled away. The Perot people had left when they heard rumors that Perot might be willing to run again. The New Party, which was in discussions with the Third Parties group but never fully on board, decided to work with the Democrats. In the end it was Green party activists who took charge of the Nader campaign, while the prospective Third Force coalition faded away and never held another conference.

There were unhappy Greens as well. A significant number of California Greens felt the receptive process had been hatched behind their backs and operated without grassroots participation. Greens nationwide saw their options for the Presidential race limited when Nader was put on the California ballot, but no one had sought any formal approval outside of that state. Greens also questioned the choice of Nader just as NIPN had. The candidate was not and did not intend to become a member of a state Green party, and he was running on a limited platform of democratic reform and corporate accountability rather than on the Ten Key Values. Come March only a quar-

---

[9] Lenora Fulani had become involved in the Patriot Party after her 1988 and 1992 Presidential campaigns as the candidate of the New Alliance Party. Fulani was regarded as an opportunist attempting to take over various organizational vehicles for her own political agenda.

ter of the California voters who were registered in the Green Party voted in the primary, a lack of participation which some attributed to a desire to dissent from the whole process of putting Nader on their ballot. Another complaint was about Steve Schmidt's platform writing for adoption at the second Green Conference in August, at which Nader was expected to be nominated by the party at large. Schmidt did solicit input from Greens via email—not the most participatory process—but adoption of his platform would negate the whole long SPAKA process of 1987-1990.

None of this deterred those on the Nader bandwagon, who were too busy to pay attention to the nay sayers. Linda Martin set up shop in a cramped ten by ten foot Washington office as the Draft Nader for President Clearinghouse running "The People's Campaign for the Presidency," while the 40-State Green Party team of Feinstein, Schmidt and Jan ran the California campaign and advised state parties petitioning to get on their states' ballots. The two coastal legs of the campaign weren't always in sync and sometimes stepped on each other, but together they managed to keep things moving forward. Both also labored under "Nader's Rules," which separated his activities from theirs. Nader continued his usual routine of giving talks, interviews and book-signings around the country, with a lot of free media coverage sparked by his role in the Presidential race, including C-SPAN coverage of some of his speeches. He also took part in campaigns for various causes, like a ballot initiative for statewide health insurance in California. But the real campaign work for Nader's Presidential run—fund-raising, filing financial reports with the F.E.C., printing and distributing literature, answering phones, coordinating volunteers, press relations, and semi-managing all of that—had to be done by independent committees without any communication or coordination with the candidate.

It was a bare-bones campaign. The Clearinghouse distributed its toll-free phone number via fliers and bumper stickers, connecting callers with other volunteers or Green party members in their states and giving advice on organizing. They used a website and email for networking, and in California Greg Jan commandeered the email list for fundraising, seven years ahead of the Howard Dean Presidential team which putatively invented internet campaigning. Nader approved putting his name on a state's ballot only when his supporters in the state had done the necessary groundwork for it. This was a complicated process, due to varying state laws about ballot access, rules for petitioning, deadlines, and (if necessary) write-in campaigns. In some states petitioners could use Nader's name in advance of his written approval, in other states petitioners had to use stand-in candidates and explain to voters that Nader would be substituted once ballot access was assured. All of them had to use stand-ins for a Vice Presidential candidate, as one had not yet been chosen. On top of the state law considerations, organizers had to be mindful of federal election laws. Pennsylvania lawyer Tom Linzey, working in close collaboration with Martin, gave pro bono legal advice to guide state campaigners through this legal maze.

The easy states were those which already had Green Party ballot lines: besides California and Maine, the Alaska and New Mexico parties soon nominated Nader as their Presidential candidate. In May petition drives in Hawai'i and Nevada succeeded in getting their parties ballot access, and by mid-July Nader was on the ballot in those states as well as in Oregon and Colorado. There were also strong ongoing petition drives in another dozen states. By the time of the August Green Conference, Nader was on the ballot in another four states: New Jersey, Iowa, Utah and Washington.

That spring and summer Mike Feinstein was busy preparing for the Green Conference, a follow-up to the previous year's Albuquerque conference, which this time was to be held in Los Angeles.[10] Just as with the first conference, Feinstein planned to put G/GPUSA on equal footing with state Green parties, GPN, and other Green groups. By now G/GPUSA in its reduced condition was dominated by left Greens in a few local chapters, such as in St. Louis, Missouri, and Syracuse, New York. Relations between the G/GPUSA

---

[10] In addition to this work and his help with the California Nader campaign, Feinstein also ran for—and won—a seat on the Santa Monica City Council that year!

leftists and the electoral activists were still testy. In December the St. Louis Greens had belatedly scheduled the Green Roundtable to meet in their city in March, the same time and place that the G/GPUSA Green Council was to meet. They had not bothered to consult with GPN or the other prospective participants. GPN publically rejected the offer, seeing it as an attempt to assert control rather than coming to the table as equals. When Feinstein attended the Green Council meeting that March he got an earful, but still he persevered in soliciting G/GPUSA attendance at the Los Angeles conference.

Greens of different views may have been divided over the Nader campaign, but they began to coalesce in discussions about a Vice Presidential nomination. Some saw it as an opportunity to mollify those uneasy with Nader, others as a way to assert Green values in the campaign. Internet discussions lit up and by mid-April there was wide agreement that the candidate should be a woman of color, a well-known Green, and an experienced activist. There was support for different candidates in different areas of the country, but in July it became known that Nader had his own candidate in mind: his friend Rob Hager, off in Kyrgyzstan. Alarm bells went off in the Clearinghouse, as this pick would violate almost all of the agreed-upon criteria. They tried sending a trusted Nader confidant to dissuade him, only to anger Nader. Then Tom Linzey took a stab, writing up a lawyerly memo laying out the pros and cons of different potential candidates, reminding Nader of his oft-stated position that this would be a citizen-led and not a candidate-led campaign, and promoting Winona LaDuke as a favored pick. LaDuke was not a Green party member, but she was an internationally-known Ojibway activist and a Harvard-trained economist with a master's in rural development. Linzey took care to acknowledge the eminent qualifications of Hager in his memo while trying to steer Nader away from him. He also put together a straw poll of over a hundred state organizers to solicit their views of the candidates, tracked down LaDuke to lobby her to accept a nomination, and tried to reach Hager to get him to back them up. Fortunately Hager had already learned what was afoot and lobbied Nader on behalf of LaDuke. When

LaDuke came in first in the straw poll she and Nader agreed to meet. They hit it off, LaDuke agreed to Nader's Rules, and the deal was sealed.

The Green Conference opened on Thursday, August 15th, at the Los Angeles campus of the University of California. Workshops and plenary sessions were scheduled for the first few days, with the Presidential nomination planned for Monday afternoon, the last day of the conference. Over the weekend Rensenbrink was repeatedly approached by people asking if there couldn't be a rapprochement with G/GPUSA while so many Greens were gathered together in one place. Among them was Jana Cutlip, the current President of the G/GPUSA Green Council. Early Sunday evening, with the G/GPUSA Green Congress scheduled to meet on Monday morning, a number of Greens had an informal discussion on the topic. Rensenbrink learned that Cris Moore, the initiator of the Albuquerque Conference and someone who had been active with the left Greens, got his New Mexico party's backing for a proposal to abolish the Congress and replace it with a new Association of State Green Parties. This surprised and delighted Rensenbrink, who immediately saw that the proposed Association was based on the Confederation of State Green Parties that GPN had been promoting. Later in the evening Rensenbrink encountered Cutlip and found they had both come up with an idea to make the proposal easier for the Congress to swallow. The idea was to amend the proposal to keep the Green Congress as an advisory body to the new Association. Moore approved the idea, so Cutlip planned to sponsor the amendment at the Congress the next morning.

When the Congress convened it immediately became tied up with challenges about procedural issues, which Rensenbrink came to believe were a delaying tactic from opponents of Moore's proposal. Finally the proposal came up for discussion. Both criticism and support were expressed, but overall the response seemed unexpectedly positive. However, the motion to move the proposal to a vote was defeated when proxy votes were cast by Don Fitz of the St. Louis chapter and Betty Wood of the Syracuse chapter.

That two people could swing a vote which was heading in the other direction struck many G/GPUSA delegates as undemocratic. When it later became known that Betty Wood, as the G/GPUSA Clearinghouse Coordinator, was also the arbiter of who was entitled to how many proxies, the heightened indignation further eroded the remaining support for G/GPUSA. And if that wasn't enough, another shoe was soon to drop.

The UCLA auditorium was decked out for the afternoon nomination session like a typical national convention with balloons, banners, and hundreds of delegates swarming the floor. Reporters came from around the world to cover the event. Representatives of over twenty-five state parties each spoke about their state's campaign and cast their nomination for Nader as President, capped off by Feinstein shouting "the Green Party nominates Ralph Nader for President!" to the expected celebratory pandemonium. More speeches were delivered, culminating in the introduction of Nader just in time for the 6 pm live broadcast on C-SPAN. Nader, who later wrote that the conference reminded him of "an Earth Day gathering," peeked around the curtains during a standing ovation and the chanting of "Go, Ralph, Go!"[11] He took the podium and began:

> Thank you very much. You must know that you were responsible for all this; all I did was accept. [*applause*] Some of the prior speakers touched on a number of issues, and as I was listening to them what occurred to me is that most of the issues and the subjects that the Green Party is adhering to are majoritarian issues in the United States of America. And this is what commended the Green Party so much to those of us who were not in on the founding is that, if you looked very carefully at the Green Party platform that's being proposed for your approval, this is by far the most

---

11 When the chant broke out again later in his speech, Nader amended it to "Go, WE, go!" The crowd took up the amended chant repeatedly during his talk, and it later became a slogan of the Clearinghouse.

comprehensive, broad-based platform that deals with a wide range of systemic justice that's needed in this country—from the political, to the corporate, to the cultural, to civil liberties, to civil rights— platform of any party in the country.

Nader went on to deliver a two-hour plus seminar on the corporate corruption of democracy and his proposals for new tools for democratic citizenship. He ended by lauding the Green Party for offering an alternative to the two parties and encouraged them:

It's the margin of difference. It's the awakening of people to issues that are taboo by the political parties. It's the recruitment of the next generation of political leaders. It's the creation and sustenance of new civic communities. If you have a multi-purpose political party, you can never lose. You can only win—in installments.

Immediately following the conference GPN held a two-day retreat, basking in the glow of their achievement in finally launching a Green Party Presidential campaign. But that other G/GPUSA shoe was about to drop. Shortly after Rensenbrink got back to Maine he received a call from Mike Feinstein, who had discovered that two weeks earlier Betty Wood had applied to the Federal Elections Commission for G/GPUSA to be recognized as the Green Party of the United States. As evidence for their electoral activity she referenced the campaigns of Nader and several Green party candidates over the last few years, including Rensenbrink's current campaign for the U.S. Senate! None of these candidates had been informed of the application, and most of them had conducted their campaigns without any connection with G/GPUSA. Rensenbrink and Feinstein knew this was another pre-emptive move to deny GPN or any new Association of State Parties a claim to be a national Green Party. They also suspected a more mercenary motive. If Nader were to reach 5% of the popular vote in the fall election, the national party which sponsored his campaign would qualify for millions of dollars in federal funding for the next Presidential campaign cycle.

This act was the decisive nudge that pushed Feinstein and many other Greens off the fence between GPN and G/GPUSA, a fence which now looked necessary rather than regrettable. Hank Chapot, whose two runs for a seat in the California State Assembly were also claimed by G/GPUSA, filed a brief with the F.E.C. contesting the application. Rensenbrink began urging Linda Martin and others involved in the Nader campaign to help organize a meeting soon after the election, before the energy it engendered had dissipated, to finally establish a national Green Party organization completely separate from G/GPUSA.

As the Nader campaign moved into the fall media attention moved on as well, relegating it to a sideshow to the main event of President Clinton versus Republican nominee Bob Dole. An exception to this media fixation on the dominant party candidates was the unsuccessful struggle of the Nader and Perot campaigns to get their candidates into the televised Presidential debates, a drama which shifted the media spotlight for a short time. Ultimately the Commission on Presidential Debates, which was and is controlled by the two dominant parties, evaded the campaigns' efforts and excluded the other candidates from the debates.

On election day Nader received 0.71% of the popular vote, coming in fourth after Ross Perot and ahead of the Libertarian and other alternative party candidates.[12] More importantly for the Greens, the Nader campaign had spurred organizing in more than forty states, gotten his name on the ballot in twenty-one states and the District of Columbia (as an independent in five of them and the nominee of the Pacific Party in Oregon), and created write-in campaigns in another two dozen states. All this organizing work was ultimately to result in the second founding of a national Green organiza-

---

[12] Perot received 8.4% of the vote, less than half his 1992 vote share. The Libertarian candidate won 0.5%.

tion—only this time unambiguously as a political party.

After much labor to accommodate various schedules, Linda Martin managed to reserve space at the historic Glenn-Ora estate in Middleburg, Virginia, for the weekend of November 16th-17th, a little over a week after the election. Glenn-Ora, which is on land surveyed by George Washington and had once hosted John F. Kennedy, was owned by the mother of Elaine Broadhead, a major contributor to the Draft Nader for President Clearinghouse. The Green parties of Maine and Connecticut put out a call to all the state campaign groups to assemble there, emphasizing that the meeting was "not about whether to form such a union of state Green parties, but is intended to proceed to its formation effectively, building on the momentum and enthusiasm generated by the Draft Nader effort in more than 40 states." Leaders of G/GPUSA, of course, disseminated their own letter opposing the meeting and its purpose. They called for state Green parties instead to attend a December G/GPUSA meeting and negotiate a unified structure. Unsurprisingly, this tired gambit had worn out its effectiveness.

On Saturday, November 16th, sixty-two Greens representing thirty-one state parties came together in Middleburg, about forty miles outside of Washington, D.C., to act on the proposal for a state party association. Although spirits were still high from the campaigns for Nader and other Green party candidates, discussion revealed some lingering reservations among the attendees. There were those who wanted to move more slowly in creating a state party association, some of whom were still concerned about relations with G/GPUSA. The long-time Greens explained to newcomers the differences between the two organizations and the long history behind their divergence. Then after dinner Rensenbrink initiated a roll call of the attendees to determine which states were ready to take the plunge. Green parties in Arizona, Arkansas, Connecticut, the District of Columbia, Maine, Nevada, Oregon, Rhode Island, Tennessee, Utah and Wyoming had empowered their representatives to join, and they voted to found the Association of State Green Parties (ASGP). Most of the others committed themselves to make a favorable recommendation to their state parties. The new association adopted provisional by-laws creating a Coordinating Committee of two delegates from each state, and they composed a statement of purpose with the twin goals of assisting in the development of state Green parties and creating a legally structured national Green Party. The long-sought goal of GPN leaders had finally come to pass.

On Sunday Ralph Nader joined them to mix with those who had campaigned for him and make a few remarks. He closed with a statement summing up a shared sentiment of those present:

> What the campaign taught us was the enormous vacuum the two major parties have left at the community level. When you're actually on the ground, you can see the Green Party has got to start driving for majority status.

Howie Hawkins also showed up at the meeting and was allowed to speak on Sunday evening. He presented his objections to little effect, his audience informing him that the founding of ASGP was already a done deal. Another blow to G/GPUSA leaders was the rejection of their application to the F.E.C., which transpired within a week of the Middleburg meeting. In typical bureaucratic reasoning, the F.E.C. decided that since Nader never registered with them as a candidate, no organization could claim that he had run as the candidate of their party. The way was clear for ASPG to aim at seeking F.E.C. recognition for itself.

Over the next few years ASPG grew quickly while G/GPUSA continued to decline. In July 2001, after a second Nader Presidential run, ASGP renamed itself the Green Party of the United States. About three months later the F.E.C. recognized GPUS as the national committee of the state Green Parties, leading the majority of the G/GPUSA members of to leave it for GPUS. As I write this GPUS has continued in existence for 24 years since that 1996 meeting.

CONCLUSION

A Strategic Dilemma

John Rensenbrink rode in the car from the airport with Ralph Nader in the back seat. It was the spring of 1997 and Nader was on his way to the Maine Green Party convention as the keynote speaker. Rensenbrink leaned back from the passenger seat in the front. "Next time, number one, we want you to run," he said. "But, number two, we want you to do it within F.E.C. rules." There was a long silence as Nader contemplated the words.

Nader did run as an official F.E.C. candidate in 2000, jettisoning the "Nader Rules" that had complicated the campaign four years earlier. He ran hard, visiting all fifty states and holding giant rallies attended by thousands, and in November obtained 2.74% of the popular vote. This was nearly four times his vote share of 1996. Nader's second run with the Greens added tens of thousands of new members to the state Green parties, helped them to win more ballot lines, and lifted hundreds of Greens to local offices. This was definitely a high point for the electoral and party–building ambitions the Greens had been harboring for many years.

Then things went downhill rapidly. That same election resulted in vicious attacks on Nader and the Green Party for playing the role of "spoiler" in a very close election between Democrat Al Gore and Republican George

W. Bush. Despite multiple arguments for why his run was not responsible for the outcome, the blame fell on him anyway and transformed Nader from a respected public figure to a political pariah. It turned Democrats and progressives against the Greens and roiled the newly renamed Green Party of the United States as it began to consider its strategy for the next Presidential election. Should they nominate Nader once more or nominate someone else to avoid the tarnish of 2000? Should they run another aggressive campaign or keep a low profile in swing states and focus on "safe" states so as not to be accused of being "spoilers" again? Or maybe avoid Presidential politics for now and just run candidates for other offices? Their contentious 2004 national convention nominated David Cobb as its candidate, who promised to refrain from campaigning in battleground states unless a state party asked him to. Nader ran as an independent due to the divisions within the Green Party. Some state Green parties backed Cobb, some backed Nader, and hard feelings were are around.

Cobb was a leader in the Green Party of Texas but was virtually unknown to the national public. In November he received one-tenth of one percent of the popular vote, a huge decline for the party from the 2000 election and one-seventh of Nader's vote share in 1996.[13] The number of Green party candidates fell, the number of electoral wins fell, the rise in Green party memberships halted, and the number of Green Party ballot lines shrank from twenty-two to fifteen. The party was rife with recriminations over the debacle and divisions over how to recover from it. The vote shares of its next three Presidential candidates illustrate its slow and painful rebuilding: 2008 nominee Cynthia McKinney 0.12%; 2012 nominee Jill Stein 0.36%; and 2016 nominee Jill Stein 1.07%.

As mentioned at the beginning of this book, I first registered as a Green Party voter in the fall of 2004 when I moved to the Bay area of California. The "spoiler" accusation regarding the 2000 election did not deter me. The

---

[13] Nader won 0.56% in 1996.

accusation seemed anti-democratic (in attacking the right of alternative parties to run candidates and the right of voters to vote for them), reductionist
(focusing on one variable to explain an election outcome when there were
dozens of important variables), and disingenuous in its claim that Nader
"stole" votes from Gore (Nader was running against the corporate corruption of democracy, which bore no resemblance to anything in the Democratic Party's platform). In talking with other Green Party volunteers before and
after the election I heard stories about the loss of members and general de-
moralization within the party due to the 2000 election and its aftermath.
The hope that the election presaged continued growth for the party proved
to be illusory—for me as well as for others—while my fears about the inevitable marginalization of the party were realized.

When I moved to Oregon two years later I briefly rejoined the Democrats, only to switch to a "non-affiliated" voter status shortly after. While
working for ranked choice voting (RCV) I met several Pacific Green Party
members in Oregon who I came to respect and registered as a Green again in
2015. In 2016 I gathered signatures for an RCV ballot initiative and ran for
statewide office on the party ballot line. I also watched with interest the
emergence and growth of the Bernie Sanders campaign in the Democratic
Party's Presidential primary. Within the Pacific Green Party we had discussions about preparing for the influx of former Bernie supporters when he
lost the primary. But when he lost and some of his supporters showed up,
we didn't have much for them to do other than to vote for our candidates in
the November election. When our Presidential candidate Jill Stein was accused after the election of being a "spoiler" in some key swing states in
which Republican Donald Trump narrowly prevailed over Democrat Hillary
Clinton, it was déjà vu all over again. Four years later in the 2020 Presidential election, which ended shortly before this book went to publication, GPUS
nominee Howie Hawkins—who, as you will recall, had once opposed the
creation of a national party and running candidates for higher offices—
obtained a measly 0.2% of the vote, wiping out the gains of the last two Pres-

idential elections.

That the "spoiler" accusation would eventually be used to stifle a growing alternative party was predictable. In European nations that elect public officials with some form of proportional representation, the "spoiler" accusation is nonsensical. That is what parties are *supposed* to do—attempt to gain votes at the expense of other parties. If an alternative party can build to an appreciable percentage of the vote for seats in a legislative body, say 5%, they would receive about 5% of the seats. That they should compete for votes is perfectly understandable; more votes equals more seats. But the United States does not have a proportional representation electoral system. It has what is variously known as the single-member/plurality, "first past the post," or "winner take all" election method, which produces a two-party system. A given electoral district elects a single office holder, whether in the legislative or executive branch, and the winner is whoever gets the most votes in the district (a plurality, not necessarily a majority). This creates an incentive for two large parties to emerge, each soaking up as many voters as possible into their coalition in order to gain more votes than their rival party. If an alternative party builds to an appreciable percentage of the vote, and its vote share is greater than the margin of difference between the winning party and the other dominant party, the alternative party will be blamed for ignoring the reality of the electoral system and "spoiling" the chances of the losing party. Particularly if the loser is the dominant party that the alternative party seems to have the most in common with. This blame and shame tactic deters people from voting for the alternative party and drives members and potential members away. It is probably the single biggest obstacle to growing an alternative party.

It would be easy to say that the Greens who pushed for creating a party should have had a strategy prepared for this. This is especially so as John Rensenbrink and many of his allies in the electoral wing of the Green movement, such as Christa Slaton and Tony Affigne, were political scientists. Rensenbrink actually recruited political scientists to the Greens through his professional association. They must have known about the "spoiler" problem. The fact that the party splintered in acrimony after the 2000 Presidential election over how to contend with the possibility of another "spoiler" election indicates that they did not have a settled strategy in place before that. Any expectation that such an election could redound to their benefit—such as by forcing the Democrats move toward their policy positions—didn't hold up to this high-profile stress test. The blame and shame tactic of the "spoiler" accusation is much easier and more attractive to the Democrats than changing their positions, unless it is merely campaign lip-service. Further evidence of a lack of a strategy may be found in the experience of the Green Party of New Mexico. In the 1990s it was probably the most successful of the state Green parties in racking up impressive vote shares for high level offices. They were then attacked as "spoilers" in the 1994 race for governor and Congressional races in 1997 and 1998, eventually leading to intra-party turmoil the same as the national party would experience after the 2000 election. Yet the New Mexico Greens did not seem to anticipate this, and no one heeded this warning bell as the party pushed forward at the Presidential level.

In the pre-2000 sources I used in my research I found no account of any discussions specifically aimed at creating a strategy for potential "spoiler" elections. This doesn't mean they did not happen, but it does indicate that the authors of those sources did not regard any such conversations as important enough to mention.[14] Yet the topic of how a new party could manage the challenges of the two-party system came up repeatedly. In the final chapter of Spretnak and Capra's seminal book *Green Politics*, which kicked off the first founding meeting, they discuss how it would be difficult to win legislative seats without proportional representation, and the consequent damag-

---

[14] I have not reviewed all of the discussions carried on in various Green Party journals and newsletters of this period. Most of the sources I consulted were in the nature of summaries and overviews of the debates among the Greens.

ing perception of alternative parties as perennial losers.[15] The electoral wing of the Greens were continually challenged by Left Greens to explain how they would avoid being co-opted or marginalized as previous alternative parties in the U.S. have been. And after the formation of GPOC in 1990, Carl Boggs's article, "Why the California Greens Should Wait to Have a Party," criticized GPOC for failing to take account of the lessons of previous alternative parties. So the topic of the problems of alternative parties in the U.S. was always in play. Those in the electoral wing acknowledged problems common to alternative parties such as ballot access laws, raising campaign money, and attracting media attention. But it seems those discussions rarely focused on ways to address the "spoiler" problem.

In trying to understand this neglect I reflected on my own actions while I was an official in the Pacific Green Party of Oregon. I am a political scientist. I knew about the "spoiler" problem. I knew how it had hurt the party after the 2000 election. Yet I didn't give much attention to developing a strategy for the possibility of such event in our state races. Why not? I think there were two principal reasons. First, there were always more immediate problems to attend to. The possibility of a "spoiler" election was just that, a possibility. In most elections the vote margins between the two dominant parties are larger than the vote share of the Green Party. So it was not as pressing an issue as others, such as keeping the party organization functioning, running campaigns, and dealing with intra-party conflicts.

Second, there was a taboo in my mind about raising the issue because it could split the party. The members of any alternative party will have at least one thing in common: they are very dissatisfied with the two dominant parties. But there will be a wide range in how dissatisfied they are. In the Green Party this comes down to the question of "just how bad is the Democratic Party?" Some would say the Democrats are worse than the Republicans, because they co-opt potential Green voters with promises they have no intention of keeping. Others say the two dominant parties are equally bad. Yet

---

[15] Spretnak and Capra (1986), p. 202-203.

others say both dominant parties are bad, but some Democratic candidates are better than most of them. And others say Democrats are not good, but usually better than Republicans. Any position the party might propose on running potential "spoiler" candidacies—whether to go ahead and do it, avoid doing it, or do it in some situations but not others—will likely start passionate arguments and end up alienating a big chunk of the coalition making up your party. Given the small size of the party and the imperative of building it, the psychological pressure to avoid such divisive issues is strong. Why spend time trying to set a strategy when there are no good options? It creates a real strategic dilemma.

These explanations could also fit the early Green electoral activists. The prospect of a high visibility "spoiler" election was, through much of that time, remote. Up through 1990 there was no Green Party ballot line in any of the fifty states, so Green candidates ran as independents and there was no party to blame for any "spoiler" scenarios. There were a minuscule number of candidates running, and almost all of them ran in local non-partisan elections, where running a truly competitive campaign is a real possibility— from 1985 through 1990, forty-six Green candidates ran and over one-third of them won. Candidates were running on Green Party ballots lines by 1992, but still most of their ninety-three candidates that year ran in local, non-partisan races. Meanwhile there were a variety of other issues to attend to. Some were practical issues regarding non-electoral projects. Some were issues of problematic patterns of behavior, such as the treatment of women within the movement. And some were tactical issues such as forming coalitions with other organizations. Addressing the "spoiler" problem was easy to defer.

But most importantly, the electoral activists' attention was primarily diverted into their protracted battle simply to win acceptance for their desire to run candidates under a Green Party label. One can imagine that if the founders had all come into the founding meeting intending to create a political party, they would have put their minds to work on ideas to overcome the obstacles of the two-party system, eventually addressing the "spoiler" problem. But most of those at the founding meeting were opposed creating a party, and in fact there was an effort to exclude people who wanted to create a party. The minority who did expect to create a party found themselves at a disadvantage, outnumbered and confronting an organized group of Murray Bookchin's followers from the ISE. Fortunately for the electoral-inclined, John Rensenbrink, who was already a experienced activist of many years standing, soon joined them and took up the cause. Meanwhile the anti-party wing became more formally organized as the Left Greens. Thus from the start there was a power struggle between two factions defending their positions on the subject. The electoral wing made the case for a party and the Left Greens made the case against a party, creating a polarized debate rather than seeking a meeting of the minds. It was not a situation conducive for the electoral wing to dwell on any weaknesses in the path they were promoting.

Two other key issues also were related to this. The debate over political ideology was not simply about which was more philosophically sound, the Left Green's socialist standpoint or the electoral wing's belief that the old left-right debates could be transcended. It was also about the electoral wing's concern over how a commitment to socialism would play in the larger voting public. They were convinced that this would guarantee a U.S. Green Party would be relegated to a fringe sect, and so they were predisposed to oppose it. The other issue was reforming the internal organizational rules. This debate wasn't simply about how best to create a more functional organization. It was also, especially later, about which of the factions would have the power to implement their preferred vision of the organization. The anti-party wing used their early advantage to hold off the electoral wing's growing influence, finally creating a structure which they could dominate. Neither of these debates were purely a matter of allies trying to find consensus on difficult questions. Both were more about factions playing offense or defense in an increasingly antagonistic situation.

In 1992 the electoral wing broke with the old organization entirely, depriving skeptics of a forum to confront the electoral leaders with questions about their strategy. Those occupied in organizing state parties and seeking ballot access had no incentive to dwell on potentially divisive issues such as how to deal with the possibility of "spoiler" situations. By this time they seem to have become immersed in wishful thinking to fuel their drive forward, downplaying likely stumbling blocks to building a party and playing up more hopeful signs. The public's growing dissatisfaction with the dominant parties, the achievement of unexpectedly large vote shares by Green candidates, and the enthusiasm among rank-and-file Greens about forming state parties were all seen as signs of the potential for continual growth. Apparently they believed this would carry their vote shares upward until they reached a point of competitiveness with the dominant parties. It may have worked, if it were not for the "spoiler" problem lurking on the sidelines. After 2000 there was no escaping the issue.

Ultimately, the only solution for the "spoiler" problem is to change the electoral system. From the start the leaders of the U.S. Greens recognized that a new party would fare better under a proportional representation system. However, there was not (and still is not) much of a prospect for instituting proportional representation in the United States. It would entail a major change in the way elections are conducted, including abolishing most electoral districts and weakening the traditional tie between an elected official and a specific geographic locality. The scale of such a change would be a very heavy lift for a group as small and politically weak as the Greens.

But fortunately for them, the hope of breaking the two-party system was a part of the larger political zeitgeist. By the 1990s there were scattered groups around the country promoting proportional representation, and in June of 1992 several of these came together and founded Citizens for Proportional Representation. They moved their office to Washington, D.C., the following year and changed their name to the Center for Voting and Democracy, indicating support for other types of electoral reforms as well. Among these was ranked choice voting. Representatives of the Center travelled the country advocating electoral reform proposals to the press and to various interested groups, including those present at the three GPN/Third Force conferences in 1993, 1994 and 1995. In 1996 the Center backed a referendum for elections to the San Francisco Board of Supervisions to use a form of proportional representation in which voters rank the candidates. It was defeated, 56-44%, but attracted lots of media attention. The next year in New Mexico, where the state Green Party had been attacked for "spoiler" elections for governor and the U.S. Congress, an RCV measure for statewide elected offices passed the state Senate. This bill was an early sign of a shift in the reformers' focus from proportional representation to the single-member district form of RCV, in which voters can rank the candidates running for a single public office. RCV in single-member electoral districts not only reduces the chances of a "spoiler" election but is a simpler reform to institute than proportional representation would be.

Ironically, the Greens' willingness to plow ahead without a strategy for "spoiler" elections helped popularize RCV as an answer to their dilemma. The 2000 Presidential election and all the hubbub about Nader being a "spoiler" accelerated interest in RCV around the nation. The Center for Voting and Democracy received national media attention from multiple outlets and RCV bills were introduced in a dozen states and the U.S. Congress. In 2002 voters in San Francisco passed an initiative to use RCV in city elections, including for their Board of Supervisors, Mayor, City Attorney, and Treasurer. It was implemented in 2004, the same year the Center for Voting and Democracy became FairVote. Since then RCV has been implemented in about two dozen cities and counties across the nation, as well as for federal elections in the state of Maine in 2020. Now Greens have a strategy for addressing "spoiler" accusations: use them as an opportunity to promote RCV as a solution to the problem. The strategy has not helped the party very much, but it certainly has helped the RCV movement. And it gives Greens the hope that with the continued spread of RCV they will eventually have a chance to grow the party without the "spoiler" albatross being hung around their neck.

The story has one more twist to it. FairVote participated in a 2014 voting reform conference in Eugene, Oregon, at which a chance conversation produced a concept for a new voting method. The new concept was modelled on RCV, but voters would give scores to candidates instead of ranking them. Mark Frohnmayer was a participant in the conversation and took up the idea, recognizing its potential to improve upon RCV. In 2018 I joined him as co-petitioner for the first voters' initiative in the world to institute STAR Voting for public elections. The initiative lost by a relatively narrow margin, but two subsequent local initiatives may yet be successful. STAR Voting, like RCV, can be used in single-member districts, but it has several advantages over RCV. [16] Interest in the concept has been spreading rapidly to other states and even other nations. In the end, the electoral Greens' determined push into Presidential elections, which for a time seemed ill-conceived, eventually resulted in not just one but two electoral reform movements addressing the "spoiler" problem. File this under "serendipity."

What lessons can be drawn from this history?

For those supporting an alternative party or contemplating the creation of a new one,[17] don't underestimate the power of the "spoiler" accusation. Even if your party's positions on issues are widely popular, you have ballot access, you run a name candidate, the media gives you attention, and you can raise real money for campaigns, none of it will be enough to get a significant number of voters to stick with you. The majority of the voters who are willing to consider independent or alternative party candidates have demonstrated this repeatedly. Once they think voters have gotten burned by

---

[16] A few of STAR Voting's key advantages over RCV are that scoring allows voters a greater ability to express their preferences between candidates than ranking does; the vote-counting process is simpler; and STAR incorporates all of voters' expressed preferences into determining the winner, not just some of them. For more information go to the Equal Vote Coalition website at equal.vote.

[17] I have in mind the Movement for a People's Party, which was organized by people who were affiliated with Bernie Sanders' 2016 Presidential run.

a "spoiler" election, they will stay with or revert to voting for the candidates of the two dominant parties. You need to confront that reality.

And for the wider circle of people would like to have more real choices in elections, the lesson is to join with those working to change voting methods. This wider circle would include voters who continue to vote for the dominant party candidates even though they are not happy with them. Without progress on the electoral reform front, we are doomed to elect only candidates from one of the two dominant parties, each of which has become dependent on big donors and corporate contributions. Reforms such as RCV, or preferably STAR Voting, are essential to free voters from this closed system and to free politicians to respond to the public's wishes instead of those of powerful financial interests.

Finally, for all of my readers, take any political advice—including mine—with a grain of salt. Sometimes when you do political work with good intentions it can produce good results, even if not exactly the results you were aiming at. Having a good strategy is important. Having good luck is even better.

BIBLIOGRAPHIC NOTES

Ch. 1. A Personal Overview. Most of this chapter is drawn from my personal memories and plenty of reading on modern American political history that I've done over the years. The paragraph on the Socialist Party is derived from the most definitive work to date, *The Socialist Party of America: A Complete History* by Jack Ross (Potomac Books, 2015). The quotation from the Green Movement Committee was taken from "History," on *Green Party US* website, <www.gp.org/history>, accessed 08/26/16. When more than one source is given for a topic in the following notes, the sources are listed in rough order of their importance as a source for that topic.

Ch. 2. The German Spark. Walljasper's story comes from his Foreword to *The Greens and the Politics of Transformation* by John Rensenbrink (R.&E. Miles, 1992). Herbert Kitschelt's anecdote about lecturing in the U.S. comes from the Preface of his book, *The Logics of Party Formation: Ecological Politics in Belgium and West Germany* (Cornell Univ. Press, 1989). There is other evidence of contemporary academic interest in the German Greens in the early '80s, e.g. Elim Papdakis, *The Green Movement in West Germany* (Crook Helm, 1984). For a very critical early assessment see Robert L. Pfaltzgraff, Jr., Kim R. Holmes, Clay Clemens, & Werner Kaltefleiter, *The Greens of West Germany: Origins, Strategies, and Transatlantic Implications* (Institute for Foreign Policy Analysis, Inc., Special Report Aug. 1983), painting the Greens as anti-liberal Romantics, susceptible to manipulation by Moscow, and "often contradictory, hypercritical of current policy, and hopelessly utopian," among other things. On the *New York Times* articles, see Kevin M. Carragee, *News and Ideology: An Analysis of Coverage of the West German Green Party by the New York Times* (*Journalism Monographs*, 128/August 1991). In their Preface to the first edition of Charlene Spretnak & Fritjof Capra, *Green Politics* (reprinted in the 2nd edition, Bear & Company, 1986), the authors characterize media coverage of the German Greens before September 1983 as predominantly "negative and inaccurate."

Sources for the emergence of Green Parties in various nations include "Green Party of Aotearoa New Zealand," on *Wikipedia*, <https://en.wikipedia.org/wiki/Green_Party_of_Aotearao_New_Zealand>, accessed 09/02/16; "PEOPLE Party," *Wikipedia*, <https://en.wikipedia.org/wiki/PEOPLE_Party>, accessed 07/10/20; "Green Party (UK)," *Wikipedia*, <https://en.wikipedia.org/wiki/Green_Party_(UK)>, accessed 07/10/2020; Per Gahrton, *Green Parties, Green Future: From Local Groups to the International Stage* (Pluto Press, 2015); and Ferdinand Müller-Rommel & Thomas Poguntke, "The Unharmonious Family: Green Parties in Western Europe," Ch. 1 in Eva Kolinsky, ed., *The Greens in West Germany: Organisation and Policy Making* (Berg, 1989). The anecdotes about the Belgians on bicycles and Germans with the dead tree are from the "Introduction" in Kitschelt (above, 1989).

There are a shelf-full of English-language books on the West German Green Party. My principal sources were Thomas Scharf, "The German Greens: a political profile," in Ingolfar Blühdorn, Frank Krause, & Thomas Scharf, eds., *The Green Agenda: Environmental Politics and Policy in Germany* (Keele Univ. Press, 1995); Helmut Wiesenthal, "The German Greens: preparing for another new beginning?" Ch. 9 of *Realism in Green politics: Social movements and ecological reform in Germany* (Manchester Univ. Press, 1993); Horst Mewes, "A Brief History of the German Green Party," Ch. 2 in Margit Mayer & John Ely, eds., *The German Greens: Paradox Between Movement and Party* (Temple Univ. Press, 1998); and Müller-Rommel & Poguntke (1989). See also Spretnak & Capra (1986).

Sources on Charlene Spretnak include Charlene Spretnak, *The Spiritual Dimension of Green Politics* (Bear & Co., 1986); the "Biography" page on her website *Charlene Spretnak*, <http://www.charlenespretnak.com/bio.htm>, accessed 09/04/16; "Charlene Spretnak," *Wikipedia*, <https://en.wikipedia.org/wiki/Charlene_Spretnak>, accessed 09/04/16; and Spretnak & Capra (1986), p. xiii-xiv, xix-xxiv, 223.

On John Rensenbrink see "About the Author" in John Rensenbrink, *Against All Odds: The Green Transformation of American Politics* (Leopold Press, Inc., 1999); and "John Rensenbrink," *Wikipedia*, <https://en.wikipedia.org/wiki/John_Rensenbrink>, accessed 09/06/16. Additional details are from personal emails from Rensenbrink to the author, 05/01/17, 05/06/17, and 05/11/17; and John Rensenbrink, "Some Notes About Me," *Green Horizon Magazine*, v. 17, n. 1, Winter/Spring 2020, p. 38. The Canadian Green meeting was on Nov. 6, 1983: Mike Feinstein, "Green Party History – Unabridged" (2016) on *Green Party US*, <http://www.gp.org/history_unabridged>, accessed 02/13/17. The quote is from Darcie Moore, "5 Questions with…Green Party Founder John Rensenbrink," on *The Times Record*, <http://www.timesrecord.com/news/2015-08-21/Front_Page/5_Questions_with_Green_Party_Founder_John_Rensenb.html>, accessed 09/06/16.

A 1983 call to the North American Bio-regional Congress can be found on the *Context Institute* website: David Haenke, "The North American Bioregional Congress," <http://www.context.org/iclib/ic03/haenke/>, accessed 09/08/16. On the initiative for a national Green meeting, see Rensenbrink (1992), p. 102; Rensenbrink (1999), p. 167; Spretnak & Capra (1986), p. 226; Charlene Spretnak, "Early Years of California Greens and their national and international Green roots," *Green Party of California,* <http://www.cagreens.org/history/early-years-roots>, accessed 09/08/16; and Michael Feinstein, "A Short History of the Green Party in the United States, 1984 to 2001" (2014), *Green Pages,* <http://greenpagesnews.org/2014/07/22/a-short-history-of-the-green-party-in-the-united-states-1984-to-2001/>, accessed 09/15/16. The quotation is from Feinstein. A few details are from a personal email from John Rensenbrink to the author, 02/20/17. See also: John Rensenbrink, *Early History of the United States Green Party, 1984-2001* (May 15, 2017); I received a pdf copy from the author in June 2017, but it is also available online at the *Green Party US* website, <https://www.gp.org/early_history>. Burton's fund raising is mentioned in Howie Hawkins, "North American Greens Come of Age: Statism Vs. Municipalism," in *Our Generation,* v. 23, n. 1, Winter 1992, p. 74, <https://s3.amazonaws.com/xlsuite_production/assets/10435353/VOL_23_01.pdf>, accessed 01/31/17. Greta Gaard, in *Ecological Politics: Ecofeminists and the Greens* (Temple University, 1998), p. 197, wrote that Burton's funds were intended for airfare for people of color but as none of those invited responded to the invitation Goldberg used the funds for ISE attendees. A list of the attendees at the founding convention can be found in Gaard (1998), p. 293, n. 10.

Ch. 3. The First Founding. Hawkins (1992), p. 69-71, put the Green Party founding in the context of previous efforts to create alternative parties. Some details on the Citizens Party come from Kirkpatrick Sale, "Greens take root in American soil," *Utne Reader,* Oct/Nov. 1985, republished from *Resurgence,* May/June 1985.

"Leafy campus" and Satin quotes are from Mark Satin, "Miraculous Birth of the U.S. Green Party's 'Ten Key Values' Statement," *Radical Middle Newsletter,* <http://www.radicalmiddle.com/ten_key_values.htm>, accessed 09/10/16, republished from *Green Horizon Magazine,* v. 9, n. 1, Fall/Winter 2012. Commentator quote is from the anonymous author of "Green organizations still struggling," *Utne Reader,* Oct/Nov. 1985, republished from *Overthrow* April/May 1985. Hawkins' views are from Hawkins (1992), p. 73-74. Mike Feinstein seconds the allegation of exclusion: "Green Party History – Unabridged." On the overrepresentation of the ISE: Rensenbrink (2017). Spretnak's quote appears in her remarks on John Rensenbrink in *Green Horizon Magazine,* v. 17, n. 1, Winter/Spring 2020, p. 37.

On the structure and name see Hawkins (1992), p. 74-77; Spretnak & Capra (1986), p.

228-229, 233; Rensenbrink (1992), p. 108-109; Rensenbrink (1999), p. 109; and Gaard (1998), p. 57-58, 197. Boyte is credited with naming the CoC in Mayer & Ely (1998), p. 200. On Bookchin: Janet Biehl, "A Short Biography of Murray Bookchin," *Anarchy Archives,* <http://dwardmac.pitzer.edu/Anarchist_Archives/bookchin/bio1.html>, accessed 11/30/17.

On the genesis of the Ten Key Values, see Satin (2012); Hawkins (1994), p. 77; Gaard (1998), p. 142-145. On Satin's background see "Mark Satin," *Wikipedia,* <https://en.wikipedia.org/wiki/Mark_Satin>, accessed 09/11/16. Satin quote is from Satin (2012). The passage on leftist reservations is from Hawkins (1992), p. 77.

Ch. 4. Fledgling Fights. The Maine Greens' discovery of the CoC founding is from Rensenbrink's email, 02/20/17. On the attrition of the founding members and Boyte's activities, see Hawkins (1992), p. 77-78. The NAGN is described by the anonymous author in *Utne Reader* (1985). On the Maine internal conflict: Rensenbrink (1992), p. 129; and Rensenbrink (1999), p. 126. Greg Gerritt's tale is found in his remarks about Rensenbrink in *Green Horizon Magazine,* v. 17, n. 1, Winter/Spring 2020, p. 27. On the Clearing House issue: Hawkins (1992), p. 78; Spretnak & Capra (1986), p. 233-234; Rensenbrink (1992), p. 109; and Rensenbrink (1999), p. 109. On the bio-regionalist positions: Feinstein (2016); and Mayer & Ely (1998), p. 203.

On the 1985-86 activities of local and regional groups: Spretnak & Capra (1986), p. xiv-xv, 234-239. On California: Mike Feinstein, "Founding of the Green Party of California," *Green Party of California,* <http://www.cagreens.org/history/founding>, accessed 03/20/17; and Sale (1985). The contemporary observer was Sale. On the 1984-86 growth of local groups: Rensenbrink (1992), p. 110; and Rensenbrink (1999), p. 110. See also Gaard (1998), p. 219-220. On the IC meeting in Boston and the elections in North Carolina and Wisconsin: Hawkins (1992), p. 78-79. On Dee Berry: Rensenbrink (1999), p. 171-172. There are conflicting accounts of exactly when Berry took over leadership of the Clearing House, late 1984 or early 1985. See the passage about her at the end of her remarks on John Rensenbrink in *Green Horizon Magazine,* v. 17, n. 1, Winter/Spring 2020, p. 9. On Maine again: Rensenbrink (1992), p. 8-9, 129; and Rensenbrink (1999), p. 126. Gerritt is named as the state legislative candidate in "History of the Green Party of the United States," *Wikepedia,* <https://en.wikipedia.org/wiki/History_of_the_Green_Party_of_the_United_States>, accessed 02/11/17. Rensenbrink (2020) also names Gerritt, p. 38-39.

On the Seattle IC meeting: Hawkins (1992), p. 78; and Spretnak & Capra (1986), p. 239. On the consensus rule: Rensenbrink (1992), p. 202-203. On the tensions leading up to the Amherst conference: Hawkins (1992), p. 79; Rensenbrink (1999), p. 169-172; and Gaard (1998), p. 175, 179-183. On the conference: Mark Satin, "Fear and Longing at the Green Gathering," *New Options,* n. 40, June 30, 1987, archived at

<http://www.radicalmiddle.com/greens1.pdf >, accessed 02/22/17; and Hawkins (1992), p. 79-81. Unattributed quotations come from Satin. The quote from the brochure is from Feinstein, "Green Party History—Unabridged." The state affiliations of participants and accompanying quote are from Jay Walljasper, "The Prospects for Green politics in the U.S.," *Utne Reader*, Sep/Oct. 1987, p. 37-39. The "fascist" epithet is reported by Rensenbrink (1999), p. 175, who added that such personalized attacks shocked him deeply. Rensenbrink's Biblical allusion, the quotes of overheard grumbling, and the quotation about locations for story swapping are from Walljasper (1987). The "three difficult hours" quote is from Rensenbrink (1999), p. 175. Hawkins' and Rensenbrink's aftermath remarks are from Hawkins (1992), p. 81 & Rensenbrink (1999), p. 175. On Rensenbrink's speech, see Walljasper's Foreword to Rensenbrink (1992).

Ch. 5. The Factions Formalize. On the positive effects of the 1987 gathering and growth of locals, see Hawkins (1992), p. 81; Rensenbrink (1992), p. 110; and Rensenbrink (1999), p. 111. On SPAKA, see Rensenbrink (1992), p. 180-182; Rensenbrink (1999), p. 174; Hawkins (1992), p. 81; Gaard (1998), p. 64-65; Rensenbrink (2017); and Feinstein, "Green Party History—Unabridged." Some details are from an email from Rensenbrink to the author, 04/19/17.

On Hawkins biography, see "Howie Hawkins," *Wikipedia*, <https://en.wikipedia.org/wiki/Howie_Hawkins>, accessed 03/02/17; "Meet Howie," *Hawkins for Auditor*, <http://www.howiehawkins.org/>, accessed 03/02/17; and "Biography," *Howie Hawkins For U.S. Senate NY Green Party*, <http://www.howiehawkins.com/2006/bio.php>, accessed 03/02/17. On the development of the Left Green Network and escalating tensions: Hawkins (1992), p. 81-83; Rensenbrink (1996), p. 170-174; and Gaard (1998), p. 96-101. On the environmental philosophy debate, see Jay Walljasper, "Social ecology vs. deep ecology," *Utne Reader*, Nov/Dec. 1988, p. 134-135; and Gaard (1998), p. 179-182, 186-187. On the California Greens: Gaard (1998), p. 101-104; Rensenbrink (1999), p. 170; "History of the Green Party of the United States," *Wikipedia;* and Feinstein, "Founding of the Green Party of California."

On the 1989 gathering: Mark Satin, "Last Chance Saloon," *New Options*, n. 60, June 30, 1989, archived at <http://www.radicalmiddle.com/greens2.pdf>, accessed 03/14/17; Jay Walljasper, "Can Green politics take root in the U.S.?" *Utne Reader*, Sep/Oct. 1989, p. 140-143; Rensenbrink (1992), p. 111, 179, 182-187, 207-208; Rensenbrink (1999), p. 111, 167, 178-179; and Gaard (1998), p. 66-68, 121, 130-131, 213. On the number of Greens who had run for or won office: Feinstein (2014), accessed 04/19/17. Unattributed quotes are from Satin. Hawkins' quotes and the LGN satisfaction with SPAKA input are from Hawkins (1992), p. 83-84. On the history of the Youth Greens: Gaard (1998), p. 117-129; on the number of LGN members present: Gaard (1998), p. 112. On Spretnak and Bookchin: Gaard (1998), p. 66; and

Biehl, "A Short Biography of Murray Bookchin." The Rensenbrink "two legs" quote is from Walljasper. On the appointment of Slaton: Rensenbrink (1999), p. 174-175. The observer was Walljasper, who also described the closing celebration.

Ch. 6. Full-Fledged Fights. On state party developments in California, see Feinstein, "Founding of the Green Party of California;" Spretnak, "Early Years of California Greens;" and Rensenbrink (2017). A video of the news reports can be seen on *YouTube*, "Green Party of California - founding meeting February 1990," <https://www.youtube.com/watch?v=3vfMamhiDOY&>, accessed 03/22/17. On Michigan, California and Maine: Rensenbrink (1992), p. 124-130; and Rensenbrink (1999), p. 124-127. On developments at the national level: Rensenbrink (1992), p. 131, 203, 208-209, 256-257; Rensenbrink (1999), p. 169, 174, 177, 179; Gaard (1998), p. 129-132; and Mike Feinstein, "John Rensenbrink Played a Key Role in Early U.S. Green Electoral Strategy," *Green Horizon Magazine*, v. 17, n. 1, Winter/Spring 2020, p. 13. The "aspiring politicians" remark is from Hawkins (1992), p. 84. On Boggs' essay: Gaard (1998), p. 223-225.

On the LGN exchanges and the Earth Day action: Gaard (1998), p. 104-110. On the number of locals paying dues in 1989: Satin (1989), p. 8. On Conti and her fund raising proposal: Rensenbrink (1992), p. 204-207; and Rensenbrink (1999), p. 175. On the continuation of the SPAKA process: Christa Slaton, letter to *New Options*, n. 72, Dec. 31, 1990, p. 7-8, archived at <http://www.radicalmiddle.com/baby.pdf> , accessed 04/15/17; Rensenbrink (1992), p. 187-188; Rensenbrink (1999), p. 174-175; and Gaard (1998), p. 68, 232-233. On the IC meetings and further complaints before the gathering: Gaard (1998), p. 68-69, 110-112; Resenbrink (1992), p. 188-192; and Rensenbrink (1999), p. 110, 175.

On the Estes Park gathering: Mark Satin, "You Don't Have to Be a Baby to Cry," *New Options*, n. 70, Sept. 24, 1990, and a special letters edition of *New Options*, n. 72, Dec. 31, 1990, archived at <http://www.radicalmiddle.com/baby.pdf>, accessed 04/19/17; Rensenbrink (1992), p. 117, 189, 191-197; and Gaard (1998), p. 69-71; 113, 131. Rensenbrink (1999) p. 205 has his "anticapitalist" characterization of the economics plank.

Ch. 7. Facedown of Forces. On the Estes Park committees and GPOC discussions, see Rensenbrink (1992), p. 131-132, 196; Rensenbrink (1999), p. 128, 173-174, 180; Rensenbrink (2017); Feinstein, "Green Party History—Unabridged." On the GCoC position on state parties: Jodean Marks, "A Historical Look at Green Structure: 1984 to 1992," *Synthesis/Regeneration*, 14 (Fall 1997); archived at http://www.greens.org/s-r/14/14-03.html>, accessed 05/22/17. On Alaska: "1990 United States Census," *Wikipedia*, <https://en.wikipedia.org/wiki/1990_United_States_Census>, accessed 05/22/17; "Anchorage Demographics," Anchorage Economic Development Corporation, <http://aedcweb.com/wp-content/uploads/2013/04/3-Anchorage%20Demographics.pdf>, accessed 05/22/17; Rensenbrink (1992), p. 131; Rensenbrink (1999), p. 127, 180; "Jim Sykes," *Wikipedia*, <https://en.wikipedia.org/wiki/Jim_Sykes>, accessed 04/26/17. On the numbers of Green candidates: Feinstein, "A Short History." On California: Feinstein, "Founding of the Green Party of California." A news report on the California petition drive can be found on *YouTube*, "Green Party of California –Mindy Lorenz, Mike Feinstein 1990," <https://www.youtube.com/watch?v=aiguz8oIvzU>, accessed 09/16/20. An interview with Lorenz is also on *YouTube*, "Mindy Lorenz – Green candidate for U.S. Congress (1990)," <https://www.youtube.com/watch?v=snLIUHDXdfc>, accessed 09/16/20. On the 1991 GPOC meetings: Rensenbrink (1992), p. 132-134, 215-216, 258-259; Rensenbrink (1999), p. 128-130, 180-181; "Ronald Daniels (politician)," *Wikipedia*, <https://en.wikipedia.org/wiki/Ronald_Daniels_(politician)>, accessed 05/22/17. On the restructuring proposals: Rensenbrink (1992), p. 110, 133, 210 257-260; Rensenbrink (1999), p. 110, 128-129, 180-181; Gaard (1998), p. 72-74, 113-115, 131-132; Feinstein, "Green Party History—Unabridged." The "self-appointed 'leaders'" quote is from Gaard (1998), p. 131.

On the problems of the IC: Rensenbrink (1992), p. 109, 202-204; Rensenbrink (1999), p. 109-110. On the Elkins meetings: Rensenbrink (1992), p. 261-265; Rensenbrink (1999), p. 109, 182-186; Hawkins (1992), p. 84-85; Marks (1997); Gaard, (1998), p. 74-77, 115-117, 132-133. Most of the quotes are from Rensenbrink (1999); Hawkins' "legitimacy" and "red-baiting" quotes are from Hawkins (1992), p. 84. A few details of the new structure vary between Rensenbrink's 1992 account and Marks (1997), such as the number of regions (eleven vs. twelve) and the number of times the Green Council was to meet each year (twice vs. three times). I have followed Gaard (1998), p. 75 in placing Daniels' speech at the Green gathering rather than at the GPOC meeting as Rensenbrink (1992), p. 262 seems to do, because Gaard used sources close in time to the event.

On state party organizing: Rensenbrink (1992), p. 128, 130, 249, 272; Rensenbrink (1999), p. 125, 176. On the further persecution of GPOC leaders: Rensenbrink (1999), p. 189-191; Rensenbrink (2017); Marks (1997); "Association of State Green Parties," Wikipedia, <https://en.wikipedia.org/wiki/Association_of_State_Green_Parties >, accessed 07/24/20. On California: Feinstein, "Founding of the Green Party of California;" Spretnak, "Early Years of California Greens."

Ch. 8. The Split. On Green support for Jerry Brown: Steven J. Schmidt, "The Founding U.S. Green Platform and First Presidential Campaign," (2004) *Green Institute*, <http://www.greeninstitute.net/node/73>, accessed 11/26/17. On Nader's biography: Ralph Nader, *Crashing the Party: Taking on the Corporate Government in an Age of Surrender* (Thomas Dunne Books, 2002), p. 17-31, 34, 36-38; "Ralph Nader," *Wikipedia*, <https://en.wikipedia.org/wiki/Ralph_Nader>, accessed 11/24/17; "Ralph Nader," *Biography.com*, <https://www.biography.com/people/ralph-nader-9419799>, accessed

11/24/17; Ralph Nader, *The Seventeen Traditions* (HarperCollins, 2007); Linda Martin *Driving Mr. Nader: The Greens Grow Up* (Leopold Press, Inc., 2000), p. 83-87. On his 1992 campaign: Nader (2002), p. 38-44; Ralph Nader, "The Concord Principles: An Agenda for a New Initiatory Democracy" (source of long quote), and "Breaking Out of the Two-Party Rut," in *The Ralph Nader Reader* (Seven Stories Press, 2000); "Ralph Nader," *Wikipedia* (above).

From Rensenbrink (1992): Nader quote, p. 106; description of composition of Greens, p.108; electoral Third Force, p. 215; alignment of strategies, p. 126; planning of Kansas conference, 132-133. On the GPN founding: Rensenbrink (1999), p. 189, 191-193; Feinstein, "Green Party History—Unabridged;" Rensenbrink (2017). On the "Rationale": Gaard (1998), p. 77, 133-134, 164-166.

On the LGN reaction: Rensenbrink (1999), p. 194. On Hawai'i and Arizona: "Ballot Status History: Green Party of Hawai'i," *Green Party US*, <http://gpus.org/other/ballotstatus/hi/>, accessed 12/06/17;" "Ballot Status History: Arizona Green Party," *Green Party US*, <http://gpus.org/ballot-status/arizona/>, accessed 12/06/17. News reports on the successful petition in Hawaii can be found on *YouTube*, "Hawaii Green Party qualifies for the ballot 1992," <https://www.youtube.com/watch?v=JyPyokNOOm0, accessed 09/16/20. Hawkins (1992) quote, p. 56. On the Minneapolis gathering: Gaard (1998) p. 76, 79-81, 167; Marks (1997); Rensenbrink (1999), p. 205; Rensenbrink (2017); Feinstein, "Green Party History— Unabridged." On the debate in *Regeneration*: Gaard (1998), p. 225-227.

On the Presidential campaigns: "United States Presidential Election, 1992," *Wikipedia*, <https://en.wikipedia.org/wiki/United_States_presidential_election,_1992>, accessed 12/05/17; Schmidt (2004); "Ronald Daniels (politician)," *Wikipedia*, accessed 11/26/17; Gaard (1998), p. 262; Nader (2000), p. 39, reprinted from Ralph Nader, "Breaking Out of the Two-Party Rut," *The Nation* (July 20/27, 1992). On Green candidates: Rensenbrink (1999), p. 195, 198; Rensenbrink (2017); Feinstein, "Green Party History—Unabridged;" Gaard (1998), p. 171. Videos of Hawai'i candidates and election night news coverage can be found on *YouTube:* "Linda Martin—Green for U.S. Senate (1992),"<https://www.youtube.com/watch?v=5_bAC6OP82o>, accessed 09/16/20; "Keiko Bonk, Hawai'i Green County Councilmember (1993)," accessed 09/16/20; "Hawai'i Green Party election success TV coverage (1992)," <https://www.youtube.com/watch?v=ZK1L-cR-AVU>, accessed 09/16/20 . On New Mexico party recognition: Gaard (1998), p. 84.

On Feinstein: "Mike Feinstein," *Wikipedia*, <https://en.wikipedia.org/wiki/Mike_Feinstein>, accessed 12/07/17; "About Michael Feinstein," *Michael Feinstein City Council*, <http://www.feinstein.org/about >, accessed 12/07/17. The year of birth is from an email from Feinstein to the author, 12/26/17. On the Santa Monica conference: Mike Feinstein, "The Green Party Ripens: Victories and Hopes," first published in *Whole Life Times*, April 1, 1993, <https://web.archive.org/web/20010222174246/http://www.feinstein.org/wlt/greenparti

esofthewest.html>, accessed 12/07/17; Rensenbrink (2017); Gaard (1998), p. 134-135. Several videos from the conference are on Mike Feinstein's *YouTube* channel, "mfeinsteintube," <https://www.youtube.com/user/mfeinsteintube/videos>, accessed 09/16/20. On the Bowdoin conference: Rensenbrink (1999), p. 196; Gaard (1998), p. 134-135 (Smith quote from p. 135); Rensenbrink (2017); Mike Feinstein, "John Rensenbrink Played Key Role in Early U.S. Green Electoral Strategy," *Green Horizon Magazine*, v. 17, n. 1, Winter/Spring 2020, p. 14.

Ch. 9. Aiming Higher. On Affigne and the confederation of state Green parties: Rensenbrink (1999), p. 189-193; author information at the end of Tony Affigne, "John Rensenbrink's Green *praxis*," *Green Horizon Magazine*, v. 17, n. 1, Winter/Spring 2020, p. 7; "rousing" quotation from Rensenbrink (2017). On further GPN events: Gaard (1998), p. 95, 135-136; Rensenbrink (1999), p. 197. On the 1994 elections: "Ballot Status History: Chronology—All States," *Green Party of the United States*, <https://gpus.org/ballot-status/chronology/>, accessed 08/15/20; Rensenbrink (1999), p. 197-199; Martin (2000), p. 67-68.

On the troubles of G/GPUSA and LGN: Gaard (1998), p. 77-79, 82-84, 95, 117, 128, 206, 215, 275-276; Rensenbrink (1999), p. 205; Schmidt (2004).

On Schmidt, the New Mexico Greens, and related proposals: Martin (2000) , p. 15-16 (Schmidt quote, p. 15); Rensenbrink (2017); Gaard (1998), p. 84; Rensenbrink (1999), p. 198, 200-201, 205-206. On Rensenbrink/Feinstein conversations and the Third Force conference: Rensenbrink (1999), p. 200-201, 206-207; Martin (2000), p. 18-19, 25; Gaard (1998) p. 136-137; archive at *Third Parties '96: Building the New Mainstream*," <http://www.ibiblio.org/spc/tp96/>, accessed 09/16/20. CNN coverage of the conference can be found on the *C-SPAN* website, "Building Common Ground," <https://www.c-span.org/video/?65492-1/building-common-ground>, accessed 09/16/20. On the Forty State email and Albuquerque conference: Gaard (1998), p. 84-86; Martin (2000), p. 15-17; Rensenbrink (1999), p. 207.

On Linda Martin: Martin (2000), p. 59- 68; Linda Martin, "Mentor and Friend," *Green Horizon Magazine*, v. 17, n. 1, Winter/Spring 2020, p. p. 35; Gaard (1998), p. 171-172 (quotes from Gaard). On Martin and Hager: Martin (2000), p. 19-23.

Ch. 10. Nader '96 and the Second Founding.

On Martin and Hager: Martin (2000), p. 22-23. On NIPS: Gaard (1998) p. 137-139; Rensenbrink (1999), p. 202-203. On the California and Maine nominations: Martin (2000), p. 23, 27; Gaard (1998), p. 87, 236-238; Rensenbrink (1999), p. 203; Nader (2002), p. 45-46 (source for Nader's statement); Feinstein (2014), accessed 09/26/20; Rensenbrink (2017), accessed 09/26/20; "Letter to Ralph Nader from California Activists," *Green Party CA,*

<https://www.cagreens.org/history/1996-nader-for-president/letter-from-activists>, accessed 10/04/20. On the Third Parties conference: Martin (2000), p. 23-27; Rensenbrink (1999), p. 203-204.

On dissent over the Nader candidacy: Gaard (1998), p. 137-139, 169, 237-239, 305 n. 116; Martin (2000) 24-25; Rensenbrink (1999), p. 202-203. On the Nader campaign: Martin (2000), p. 3-6, 28-34, 46-55; Gaard (1998), p.237, 239-240; Nader (2002), p. 46-48; Ralph Nader, "The Greens and the Presidency: A Voice, not an Echo," *The Nation*, July 8, 1996, p. 16-20. The dates by which particular state parties got Nader on their ballot was constructed from partial accounts in different sources; there may be errors.

On the Green Conference: Rensenbrink (1999), p. 207-210; Martin (2000), p. 58-59, 68-69; Nader (2002), p. 48; Gaard (1998), p. 241. Quotes from Nader's speech are from *YouTube*, "Ralph Nader green party nomination acceptance speech (1996)," <https://www.youtube.com/watch?v=VwNmfBuop0g>, accessed 10/12/20. On the G/GPUS application to the F.E.C.: Rensenbrink (1999), p. 210-212; Lawrence M. Noble, N. Bradley Litchfield, & Michael G. Marinelli, "F.E.C. Agenda Document #96-113," <https://www.fec.gov/files/legal/aos/68039.pdf>, accessed 10/11/20; Martin (2000), p. 121.

On the Presidential debates and end of the campaign: Martin (2000), p. 44, 71-80, 101, 108; Noble, Litchfield & Marianelli, n. 2; "1996 United States presidential election," *Wikipedia*, <https://en.wikipedia.org/wiki/1996_United_States_presidential_election>, accessed 10/01/20. On ASGP founding: Patrick Mazza, "Reinvigorated by Nader campaign, U.S. Greens gather to plan next steps," (1996), *Green Party US* <https://www.gp.org/1996_founding_meeting >, accessed 10/26/20; Martin (2000), p. 105-108, 110, 113-114 (Nader quote on p. 113); Rensenbrink (1999), p. 32-35, 211-213; Rensenbrink (2017). On G/GPUSA and ASGP after the Middleburg meeting: Rensenbrink (1999), p. 214-220.

Conclusion: A Strategic Dilemma.

Rensenbrink anecdote is from Martin (2000), p. 102. On Nader's 2000 campaign: Nader (2002); "Ralph Nader 2000 presidential campaign," *Wikipedia*, <https://en.wikipedia.org/wiki/Ralph_Nader_2000_presidential_campaign>, accessed 10/27/20; Dean Myerson, "A Response to Miller and Hill," in Howie Hawkins, ed., *Independent Politics: The Green Party Strategy Debate* (Haymarket Books, 2006), p. 198; Alan Maas, "The Green Party's Step Backward," *Socialist Worker* (July 2, 2004), reprinted in Hawkins, ed. (2006), p. 156-157. For arguments against the "spoiler" accusation: Tim Wise, "No More Mister Fall Guy: Why Ralph Nader Is Not To Blame For 'President' Bush," republished from *ZNet* (Nov. 9, 2000), *Tim Wise*, <http://www.timwise.org/2000/11/no-more-mister-fall-guy-why-ralph-nader-is-not-to-blame-for-president-bush/>, accessed 10/27/20; Sam Smith,

"Nader Not Responsible for Gore's Loss," republished from *Progressive Review's Undernews* (July 2002), *The Progressive Review*, <http://www.prorev.com/green2000.htm>, accessed 10/27/20; Irene Dieter, "Dispelling the Myth of Election 2000: Did Nader Cost Gore the Election?" *City of Ameda Green Party*, <http://www.cagreens.org/alameda/city/0803myth/myth.html>, accessed 10/27/20; Howie Hawkins, "The Green Party's Missed Opportunity in 2004—and the Opportunity Still at Hand," Hawkins, ed. (2006), p. 29. The Hawkins volume is an invaluable resource on the strategic debates among Greens and progressives leading up to and immediately following the 2004 Presidential election; the writings in it continue to be relevant to the strategic dilemmas of third parties in the U.S. electoral system. On the results of the Cobb campaign: Hawkins, "The Green Party's Missed Opportunity," Hawkins, ed. (2006), p. 37-38.

On Stein as spoiler: Bob Bryan, "'A TERRIFYING NIGHT': Paul Krugman goes on epic tweetstorm," (Nov. 8, 2016), *Business Insider*, <https://www.businessinsider.com/paul-krugman-tweetstorm-2016-election-2016-11>, accessed 11/12/2020; German Lopez, "Green Party candidate Jill Stein got more votes than Trump's victory margin in 3 key states," (Dec. 1, 2016), *Vox*, <https://www.vox.com/policy-and-politics/2016/12/1/13811344/jill-stein-clinton-trump-nader-spoiler >, accessed 11/12/2020; "Jill Stein: Democratic Spoiler or Scapegoat?" (Dec. 7, 2016), *FiveThirtyEight*, <https://fivethirtyeight.com/features/jill-stein-democratic-spoiler-or-scapegoat/>, accessed 11/12/2020; Jonah Walters, "Can They Count?" *Jacobin*, <https://www.jacobinmag.com/2016/11/election-clinton-trump-stein-johnson-spoiler/>, accessed 11/12/2020. Hawkins 2020 vote share: "Presidential election 2020," *Ballotpedia*, <https://ballotpedia.org/Presidential_election,_2020>, accessed 11/10/2020; Abby Weiss, "Howie Hawkins unsurprised by election results, hopeful for Green Party" (Nov. 11, 2020), *The Daily Orange*, <http://dailyorange.com/2020/11/howie-hawkins-unsurprised-election-results-hopeful-green-party/>, accessed 11/12/2020.

On Rensenbrink's recruitment of political scientists: Ted Becker, "Pathfinder Toward a Transformational Politics," *Green Horizon Magazine*, v. 17, n. 1, Winter/Spring 2020, p. 9-10. On the New Mexico "spoiler" attacks: Jack Uhrich, "New Mexico: A Sobering Lesson for Practical Fusion," reprinted from *Green Horizon Quarterly* (Fall 2004) in Hawkins, ed. (2006), p. 235-243; Martin (2000), p. 110-113.

On the voting system reform movement: "Voting and Democracy Review" (n. 15, June 2002), *FairVote Archives*, <http://archive.fairvote.org/e_news/annivnwsltr.htm>, accessed 11/14/2020; "FairVote," *Wikipedia*, <https://en.wikipedia.org/wiki/FairVote>, accessed 11/14/2020; "What's Your Preference?" (Oct. 23, 1996), *SFWeekly*, <https://www.sfweekly.com/news/whats-your-preference/>, accessed 11/14/2020; "San Francisco Successfully Uses Ranked Choice Voting for Citywide Elections, Nov. 2005, <http://www.sfrcv.com/>, accessed 11/21/2020; "Our Story," *FairVote*, <https://www.fairvote.org/our_story#fair_elections>, accessed 11/21/2020. I learned the

Alan F. Zundel

STAR Voting origin story from conversations with Mark Frohnmayer.